The Squares of Islington

Part II:

Islington Parish

by

Mary Cosh

MA, FSA

Islington Archaeology & History Society

1993

ISBN 0 9507532 6 2
Printed by Henry Ling Ltd., The Dorset Press

CONTENTS

LIST OF ILLUSTRATIONS

Figs 2, 3, 23, 36, 41 and 48 are from the 1871 Ordnance Survey; fig. 6 is a detail from Ruff's 1840 map of London.

ACKNOWLEDGMENTS

As with Part I of this book, I am grateful to the many people who have given me invaluable help. Alec Forshaw, Islington Borough Conservation Officer, and Matthew Saunders, Secretary of the Ancient Monuments Society, have kindly read the complete text and made useful suggestions and amendments. I am also greatly obliged to the Most Honourable The Marquess of Northampton for reading the three Canonbury squares and Compton Terrace, as did Mr Peter Vickery of P. J. Broomhall and Partners, and Harley Sherlock, who made some important points on Canonbury Square; Rachel Bower for reading all eight Barnsbury squares, and especially for sorting out confusion on Cloudesley Square and giving me a vital reference which proved the key to research on Barnsbury Square; Mr D. E. Wickham of The Clothworkers' Company for reading and suggesting corrections on The Company's squares, Arlington, Union and Wilton, and Harry Brack for reading and commenting on Gibson Square and Packington Square. The research done by Frank Kelsall and the late Susan Beattie for the then GLC Historic Buildings Division, and in 1991 by Edward Chaney for English Heritage, proved invaluable in writing the entries on Colebrooke Row/Duncan Terrace and on the Milner-Gibson estate.

The late Sir High Wontner, who unfortunately died while this book was at the printers, and Mr Giles Wontner, were both helpful on Tibberton Square, built by their ancestor; and Miss Charlotte Mittens, archivist to the Peabody Trust, kindly read Peabody Square and supplied missing information. Julia Melvin, who read the items on the Highbury terraces and Highbury Crescent, gave useful information, and Pamela Willis, Curator of the Museum of the Order of St John, and Sid Holyland, of Angel Improvement Trust, both read and made helpful suggestions on Colebrooke Row and Duncan Terrace. Mrs M. Huxstep, Secretary of the Charles Lamb Society, gave important leads on the (still unsolved) mystery of Lamb's Cottage in Duncan Terrace.

Yasmin Webb and the staff of the Islington Central Library Local History Department, the staff of the Greater London Record Office and Library, and John Phillips of its Prints and Drawings Collection, and the staff of the Guildhall Library have all given much appreciated help and support throughout long periods of research for this book. To them I owe a great debt of gratitude.

Thanks are due to the following for permission to reproduce illustrations from their collections: The Greater London Record Office for the cover illustration, figs 2, 3, 23, 36, 41, 48 reproduced from the 1871 Ordnance Survey, fig. 6 from Ruff's map of 1840, and figs. 9, 30 and 31 from the Middlesex Deeds Register, together with figs. 8, 10–13, 17, 20–22, 26, 29, 33, 42, 53, 55 (photographs by Godfrey New). English Heritage for fig. 43. Royal Commission on the Historical Monuments of England (RCHME) Crown Copyright for fig. 4. Islington Central Library, Local History collection for figs. 1, 5, 15, 16, 18, 19, 25, 27, 28, 32, 34, 35, 38–40, 44–47, 49–52, 54. Figs. 7, 24, 37 were photographed by Pauline Lord, and the map at the end was drawn by Catherine Silver, both of whom have my thanks.

PREFATORY NOTE TO ISLINGTON'S SQUARES

Islington, long renowned for pleasure spots and recreational gardens, has become ironically enough the part of London least provided with public open space or wild-life habitats. On the other hand, it is probably the best area to study London's Regency-style houses, for thanks to the rapid outward spread of the railways in the mid-19th century, fashion left it behind only a generation after much of it was built. The new suburban middle-class who had moved into the terraces built in the 1820s and 1830s now followed London's flood-tide to ever-spreading perimeters, leaving Islington and Clerkenwell – but not high and dry, for the less prosperous classes then moved in. Houses became sub-divided into small tenements, and no capital was spent on modernising them. Now, after one-and-a-half centuries, many of those that survive have been restored to look rather as they did when new, probably smarter. Although many have gone, such large chunks of late-Georgian and Regency domestic buildings as are to be seen in Islington are a rare find in London.

INTRODUCTION

The boroughs of Islington and Finsbury, welded together rather than merged under the London Government Act of 1965, present a strong contrast. While Islington and Clerkenwell both grew up on manorial land, Clerkenwell was the seat of monastic houses – the Priory of St John of Jerusalem and the Nunnery of St Mary's – whereas Islington's estates were predominantly rural, the country manors of Bernersbury and Canonbury, respectively the property of the powerful Berners family and the Canons of St Bartholomew's, Smithfield, with the Highbury farmlands belonging to the Priors of St John. After King Henry VIII's confiscation of monastic property in 1540, Clerkenwell became the home of courtiers and other rich families; in the next century successive disasters, the Great Plague of 1664–5 and the Fire of London in 1666, brought about an increasingly urban setting with the migration of craftsmen, artisans and tradesmen from the ravaged city to this area undamaged and still largely undeveloped, adjoining it to the north; while its fashionable families moved westwards to be nearer the restored Stuart court. Before the end of the century Clerkenwell's skilled industrial character became fixed with the further influx of Huguenots escaping persecution, when Louis XIV revoked the Edict of Nantes in 1685.

Islington, meanwhile, had remained a rural village, though its position as first staging post on the main road to the north, and its proximity to the great cattle market at Smithfield, made it grow rapidly; yet it retained its village characteristics of a broad market high street, village green, mediaeval parish church on the high road, and generous scattering of noble houses. More than a mile of open fields separated it from the city, so that its manorial estates remained agricultural, split between such owners as the Earls of Northampton, the Fisher and Fowler families on the Canonbury lands, Milner-Gibsons, Thornhills and others in Barnsbury.

Only in the early 19th century did this pattern change. While Clerkenwell was becoming increasingly industrialised, Islington became a desirable site for a new, semi-rural suburb, thanks to expanding London's relentless outward pressure. Industrial Clerkenwell, still with open land belonging to the Northamptons and the New River Company on its northern fringe, could accommodate a certain amount of 'estate-into-suburb' development. For Islington this was to be by far the most common form of growth.

Starting from scratch, then, the explosion of housing round Islington village did not display the extraordinary range of either origin or building period found in Clerkenwell and Finsbury, where already in the 18th century streets and squares sprang up on old sites, dictating the appearance of the early Charterhouse and St John's Squares. In Islington, with more room for expansion, however, the period of 19th-century square-building lasted longer, until the fashion petered out altogether in favour of rows of semi-detached or free-standing villas, characterising northerly

1

expansion from the 1860s onwards (Tollington, Holloway, Tufnell Park). First to evolve was Canonbury, thrown together in random fashion from 1806 – somewhat in the manner of Claremont Square in Pentonville; last was the northern-most, Arundel, in the 1850s, even more random and never completed because of the railway's intrusion along its south side.

Most Islington squares are associated with development of an estate, of which Canonbury is the most distinguished as well as the earliest, with its contemporary, Compton Terrace. Next came Cloudesley Square in the small Cloudesley estate, marching with the slightly later Milner-Gibson estate with its two eponymous squares; Lonsdale Square on Drapers' Company land, and latest of Barnsbury's major developments, Thornhill Square on the Thornhill estate. On the other side of the High Street and Lower Road, the Clothworkers'/Packington estate provided Arlington and Union Squares and the neighbouring Wilton Square, all relatively late.

Odd ones out are Barnsbury and Arundel Squares, Tibberton adjoining the Packington estate, and the now vanished Edward Square. In the matter of lost squares Islington has fared better than Clerkenwell and Finsbury; others were Adelaide and Norfolk Squares, which seem hardly to have existed other than as a concept.

Included in this survey are terraces which can boast some of a square's elements. Among the earliest and most notable are, of course, Highbury Place and Terrace (1776 and 1789), the proto-development in Islington, either of which – had their creator not gone on to other ventures – might have launched the vogue as 'Highbury Square'. Even earlier are the unplanned Colebrooke Row and Duncan Terrace straggling like an elongated 'two-sided square' with (originally) the semi-rural New River between; later are Annett's Crescent in Essex Road and Malvern Terrace in Barnsbury, both fronted by garden ground.

Although these are not 'squares' in the accepted sense, the criterion for inclusion has been that places either call themselves 'squares', or consist of houses or terraces built – usually piecemeal – alongside existing open ground, like the examples quoted above. Almshouses, surviving or demolished, have been omitted by definition – though they would prove a fruitful subject of research. The Greens, Clerkenwell, Islington, Newington, have a special origin and purpose, and will be the subject of a separate study. Other pieces of ground created as 'open spaces' by demolition of old streets or rows, or 'closes' built on old undeveloped ground are not, there-fore, included unless they impinge on a square (e.g. Wontner Close off Tibberton Square). Hence Packington Square, self-styled, is in, but not Orchard Close, a neat single-storey Council sheltered housing development on old orchard ground (which many residents would have dearly liked to keep as it was), in the space contained behind Morton and Ecclesbourne Roads and Halliford and Rotherfield Streets; nor is the recreational space between Council flatted housing in the nearby

2

Morton Road/Queensbury St/Ecclesbourne Road. Also not included are the much earlier gardens at the Caledonian Road end of Penn Road, a residential area of expansive early-1860s villas, where an ornamental space was created by dividing the road into two at the end. Had this claimed to be "Penn Square" it would have qualified as by far the most northerly in Islington – but by that period the 'square' concept had given way both architecturally and in landscaping to a more varied and spacious style.

Still other terraces are included here for the gardens forming an integral part: Compton Terrace (actually part of the original Canonbury Square development), Annett's Crescent in Essex Road, Colebrooke Row and Duncan Terrace, facing each other across the New River channel, and the pretty Malvern Terrace. Aberdeen Park, another enclave, might well rate inclusion for its development of the square concept in a period already abandoning the idea, but was finally omitted as it does not incorporate a communal garden.

Two late-comers to claim the title by some stretching of the meaning are both in Canonbury: Alwyne Square, like Claremont Close in Pentonville more of a precinct than a square proper; and the modern John Spencer Square, the principle turned inside-out. Latest of all comes the ghost of the idea in other forms: Cornwallis Square in Holloway, which trundles out the trappings without a clear idea of what it is all about; Packington's ranged blocks of flats, a forlorn endeavour to evoke a tradition on the wrong scale and in the wrong terms – and the joky 'Angel Square', where the name is quite anomalous.

*　　*　　*　　*

Paradoxically, Islington's true squares are few: most are variants. These include:

1) two facing terraces (Tibberton)
2) isolated terraces (Canonbury, Arundel) (and in Clerkenwell, Wilmington, Claremont)
3) one hexagon – a collection of detached villas and terraces with flattened angles (Cloudesley)
4) two designed as entities in bizarre architectural form (Lonsdale, Milner)
5) one not adding up to a square at all (Barnsbury)
6) one that never was (Highbury)
7) one triangle (Wilton)
8) one in 'hippodrome' form, with detached crescents forming its end terraces (Thornhill)
9) others using square as a courtesy title (Alwyne – originally Canonbury Park Square – an enclave ranged round a central space), or John Spencer Square; Adelaide and Norfolk, barely even entities.

Alwyne Square (1857–63; 1954)

Alwyne Square occupies a confined space enclosed by streets in the Marquess of Northampton's Canonbury estate, rather after the manner of Barnsbury Wood on the Thornhill estate. It was more accessible, however, and thus apt for development, and in 1857 there began the building of an irregular circle of villas in gardens named Canonbury Park Square. In 1879, doubtless to end an irritating confusion with Canonbury Square, it was renamed Alwyne Square, matching the crop of Alwynes already built and using one of the Marquess's subsidiary family names.

The builder was Charles Hamor Hill, who in 1837 had taken a lease of Canonbury Tower from the then Marquess of Northampton, Spencer Alwyne Compton, with an agreement to make three new roads in the still open space between Hopping Lane, Canonbury Tavern and the New River. The layouts were to be completed within eight years and at least 25 houses within 21 years. By 1850 Hill had raised nearly 50 substantial, mostly free-standing villas in Canonbury Park North and South and Grange Grove. In December 1857 be obtained permission to build under the same conditions on the land abutting on Canonbury Park North, and the cul-de-sac square was the result.

In October 1859, by agreement with the Marquess, Hill sold his development for £2,400, to Henry Witten, a stockbroker, of 5 Alwyne Road, Witten taking over responsibility for building, and the new square was completed in 1863. [GLC HBC Isl. 6]

The plan accompanying the 1857 agreement showed the proposed square as consisting of ten groups forming 21 large villas, mostly in pairs, but one detached and two sets triple.

This completed the development of the "Alwyne" area of Canonbury estate. The site dictated that the new "square" — a courtesy title in view of its irregular shape — should have only one entry, from Canonbury Park North. In 1928 the Royal Commission on Squares regarded the layout as "unsatisfactory", but assumed that in 1936, when the leases fell in, it would be "ripe for development". There was talk of making a second exit to Grange Grove, so that the then Lord Northampton was unwilling to commit himself to keeping it as open space. The war intervened, however, when the houses and adjoining streets were partly destroyed by bombing; and like Canonbury Park South, the square was rebuilt in 1954 in a timid sub-classical style designed by Western Ground Rents' surveyor Nash. A single original house remains, the Coach House on the north side. The central area still contains some mature trees.

The square now consists of small blocks of flats, and a couple of rows of pastiche Regency-style houses, Grice Court running the full range of its south side. (William Grice, who died in 1953, was architect of the police flats in Canonbury Park South.)

Angel Square (1991)

Angel Square is not, of course, a square, but then it had to be called something, and "Square" has distinguished connections. Until 1990 the NE corner of the Angel, shabby but characterful, included the Art Deco "Blue-coat Boy" – though idiotically renamed "The Blue Angel", a feeble pun even less justified than "Angel Square". The whole corner was demolished in 1990 to make way for an office development designed by the architects Rock Townsend for BICC Developments in conjunction with Charlecote Estates, and completed in 1991.

Mysteriously, the new building rose to seven floors in places. The rot had set in when the undistinguished Royal Bank of Scotland, successor to the handsome Victorian Grand Theatre façade, insidiously crept to seven storeys when the public had been led to expect five. This opened a highway down which nothing like as welcome as a coach and four was driven: Angel Square, heralded at public meetings as "to be lower than the Royal Bank", somehow ended up just as high and much more massive. It is admittedly also a lot more original. "Witty", say those inclined to architectural jargon. Others find the joke a bit black. No kind of architectural gimmick, it seems, is not loaded on this heavy corner, circular on the angle, Italianate clock tower above, sudden gable terminating a kind of bow, protruding bays on the west, several varieties of brick and reconstituted stone and several kinds of fenestration, and all sorts of detail half worked in: a bit of an arch, a sort of profile obelisk, what seem like the buttresses to a fortress. So where's the square, one may ask. That's inside.

The enclosed space contains an obelisk, designed by Kevin Jordan to commemorate the very brief stay of Tom Paine in the area when writing Part I of *The Rights of Man* in 1791. He was a Norfolk man, only temporarily visiting Islington. The rest of the book was written in Paris.

Annett's Crescent (1822–6); Ridley's Factory, and Barossa Place (246–90, 292 and 294–300 Essex Road)

The stylish little Annett's Crescent of 23 houses is unique in Islington, if not altogether. It was built on a strip of land by the Lower Road, acquired by Thomas James Annett from the land-owner Thomas Scott, close to the New North Road. The architect was William Burnell Hué, of whom practically nothing is known save that from 1801–9 he was a pupil or assistant of William Jupp, junior, who was architect to four City Companies and also district surveyor to several east London parishes. [Colvin] When Annett's Crescent was begun Hué was living in Bloomsbury, and is recorded as having designed the "grand quadrangle" in front of Carlton House. His Islington crescent certainly has touches of a rather Cubitt-like ingenuity.

Dent's Plan of 1805/6 shows one large meadow of Scott's (plot 826) – whose site is now bounded by Rotherfield Street and Northchurch Road – as extending southwards to the Rosemary Branch, an old tea-garden at the parish's extreme limit; at the NW of the field a tiny sliver of land is marked off, which was later to accommodate Annett's Crescent.

The stratum of red or brickmaker's clay occurring below Islington proved very lucrative in the great 1820s building boom. Much of Thomas Scott's land along the Lower Road towards Ball's Pond was dug up to become extensive brick-fields. The limit of building at this time was James Street (now Elmore Street), just short of the brick-field. The 1819 rate books show only five houses here, three of them in Annett's name but two empty, his own being far the largest and rated double. By 1820/21 all five are occupied; in 1821 Scott's name appears, rated for stables and land – the latter doubtless the brick-field site. In 1822 these six houses are named Barossa Place, of which one is owned by Thomas Wontner of the new Tibberton Square, and Samuel Ridley's linoleum manufactory appears. In the same book, Annett's Crescent is first named, with three houses, all empty and evidently new. By 1825/6 these are occupied, and seven more are built.

This far-flung Islington outpost, bordering on the country, took on a curiously industrial aspect with its brick-field and several factories. Ridley's had been built on Thomas Scott's land in 1812, originally for Mr W. Weaver, then passed to Charles Pugsley, and in 1819 was bought by Ridley, one of the trustees of St Mary's parish, and opened as a floor-cloth manufactory. Ridley, described variously as "upholsterer, worksman and floorcloth manufacturer", and subsequently his son, held it in successive partnerships – with Ellington and Whitley – until 1893. It was then acquired by Mr A. Probyn, a beer bottler, whose own firm, founded in 1791, continued here until 1962, merging in 1958 with W. M. B. Foster & Sons to become Foster Probyn Ltd. In 1962 the family brewers Young & Co. took over, but shortly outgrew the premises and in 1972 removed to Wandsworth. Islington Council then took over and restored the pristine elegance of the exterior and converted the building to the Borough's Housing Offices.

Ridley's factory was distinguished enough – and manufactories were few enough – to merit a mention in Cromwell's *Walks through Islington*. Alongside it a path (now Halliford Street) traversed Scott's large field, leading straight to the Rosemary Branch, most of whose site was now an important white-lead works, their two impressive windmills visible from Ridley's corner. A few years later Mr Wontner founded his fur factory and not far away built Tibberton Square (q.v.).

Ridley moved to a villa in Barossa Place, next door to his works and just short of the brickfields. In 1836 Mr John Perkins, a Surrey gentleman, established a 15-acre market on a large part of the fields, in an attempt to divert the cattle trade from Smithfield and thus end the squalid invasion of herds of beasts through central London. He was defeated by the City's and land-owners' vested interests, and

Ridley's Floor-cloth Factory
showing the end of Annett's Crescent
From a water-colour of *c.* 1840 by F. N. Shepherd

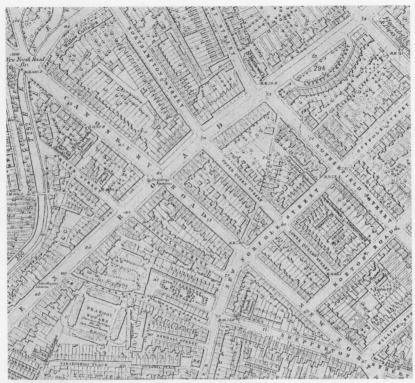

Essex Road area in 1871
Peabody and Tibberton Squares, Annett's Crescent (top right), and Adelaide
Square (bottom, south of Shepperton Street). Norfolk Square, east of New
Norfolk Street, is not marked

when Smithfield was at last moved 20 years later, an initial attempt to revive
Perkins's market (1855) was abandoned, and it moved instead to Copenhagen
Fields. Perkins's site was shortly laid out as Northchurch, Englefield and
Ockendon Roads.

All in all it is gratifying that Annett's Crescent has survived through the chequered
fortunes of this part of Essex Road. In the 1970s the Council rescued and restored the
houses, and rehabilitated the strip of garden in front. The latest London maps spell
the name "Annette Crescent", which, if not a careless misreading, ranks with the
brewers' irrelevant alterations of the traditional names of old pubs.

Architecture

The order of building Annett's Crescent seems to have been centre first (three houses), then pavilion ends, then infilling the rest. The crescent is in symmetrical terrace-form, the three centre houses slightly advanced, with 'pavilion' blocks of three at each end, the outermost houses with side entrances, no. 294's in a small extension. The houses are stuccoed throughout, ground floors in simulated ashlar, with all ground-floor features round-headed. Front door and window positions are reversed at the house near the centre, making a lopsided effect.

Unusually for Islington the upper floors have single windows, in shallow segmental recesses, with narrow cill bands between and flat parapet above, originally balustraded. First-floor windows are 4-light, floor-length, with simple window-guards, and the top floor — uniquely for the area — are small casements with margin panes. The pavilion ends have balconies with unusual decorative wheel-like motifs. Fanlights are simple, circle and flat teardrop; most ground-floor glazing is now plain.

Altogether Annett's Crescent resembles no other contemporary survivals in Islington, except some of Cubitt's to a certain extent, like Manchester Terrace (nos. 200–62 Liverpool Road), though some of the early surrounding streets have nice variants on the terrace form, such as Rotherfield Street (begun 1826). Apart from Charlton Crescent of 1791, Annett's is the only early crescent in the parish.

Ridley's Factory and Barossa Place

Although there is no justification for including these buildings apart from their proximity to Annett's Crescent, the temptation to include so dignified an industrial neighbour is irresistible. The tall four-storey Palladian building, pedimented and balustraded above an Ionic pilastered front, was originally without openings above the circular-headed windows on the ground floor, except for a single thermal window just below the parapet. It was disfigured, however, by a mass of written advertisement all over its blank walls, with Ridley's name at the top in place of a frieze, and a string of the items which might issue from its interior to customers' order: "Virander* Awnings and Portable Rooms", to say nothing of orders for the Royal Family. In this century, when it was a bottling factory, the ugly lettering had given way to two picturesque giant ale and beer bottles, one on either side. At its restoration, many people saw these removed with some regret. It has now been provided with Georgian-style windows on the first and second floors, and the classical porch which formerly adorned the entrance has long been removed. The fine balustrade adorned with stone balls has fortunately survived.

*The mis-spelling may not have been Ridley's but that of C. Barrow, a keen local water-colourist who assiduously if pedestrianly recorded many Islington buildings in 1824 and 1825.

Barossa Place consisted of half-a-dozen pretty bow-fronted semi-detached villas with small gardens in front, named after a Thomas Barossa. Ridley's house was Barossa Lodge, no. 294 Essex Road. A contributor to the *Sydney Morning Herald* in September 1961 (Edward Robinson) recalled living there with his father, Malachi Joseph Robinson, an Irish doctor, from 1906–1911, when the house had a brass lion's-head knocker, bell-pull, and large lamp above, with a brass speaking-tube which connected with his father's bedroom. This contraption was known as the Medical Man's Midnight Friend. The house was full of ornaments and weapons brought by his father from India, and in the back garden among other joys was a century-old mulberry tree. Returning to his boyhood home in 1961 was a melancholy experience: the house abandoned, dirty, peeling paint and wallpaper, the bay-window veranda gone – fallen down in the blitz, said a kindly old lady he met there. Of the mulberry only a stump remained. "No willow tree, either, no lawn, no red gravel paths, no conservatory, no strawberry beds. Nothing but an ugly brick factory building which had taken over half the garden."

In 1962 this dismal saga ended with demolition of the four houses, to be replaced by considerably higher Council flats sited without reference to the street-line.

Arlington Square and the Clothworkers' Estate

(See also Union Square, Wilton Square and Packington Square)

In mediaeval times the south-easterly quarter of Islington parish – east of the present Essex Road – formed part of the Prebend Estate of the Dean and Chapter of St Paul's; and barring a short period during the Commonwealth, the lordship of the manor remained in the cathedral's hands. At the time of Henry VIII's confiscation of ecclesiastical property, the Clothworkers' Company acquired some 34 acres of this land (known as their Corporate Estate), and in 1563 they inherited 60 adjoining acres to the west, with certain charities attached, under the will of Dame Alice Packington, whose husband Sir John had been Clerk to the Court of Common Pleas.

The open ground was near "Islington Common" on the northern fringe of Finsbury Fields, never enclosed because archery had been practised there since mediaeval times. It was dotted with archery targets in the form of 'rovers', decorated wood or stone posts each bearing some carved device, allotted such fanciful names as "Marquis of Islington", "Duke of Shoreditch", and so on. One survivor is displayed at the Honourable Artillery Company's headquarters off the City Road: Several existed well into the 19th century, and the last one known in Islington (another survived in Hoxton, see below) was, says Tomlins, actually "fixed and preserved in the brick-work of the Canal Bridge, above the towing-path". This marker was known, rather tamely, as "Scarlet". Another near "the Pathway Canal Bridge" in "Britannia Fields" had been wantonly broken up in 1842, while a third, "Jehu",

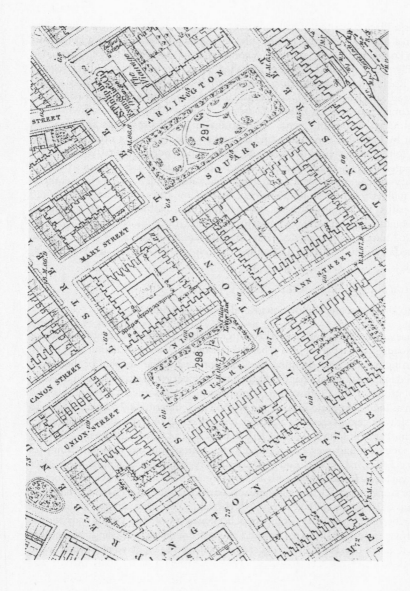

Clothworkers' and Packington estates in 1871 showing Arlington and Union Squares; Packington Street and other streets demolished for building of the Packington Square estate bearing the date 1679, was recorded until about 1853 in a field west of New North Road, but then (says Tomlins) "either removed or buried ... in constructing the buildings at Arlington Square". Its site was pinpointed as the garden of no. 24 Arlington Street. Until the estate building began it was visible in the open field just after crossing the bridge. And on the Hoxton side of the New North Road, also near the canal bridge, still surviving in 1858 was "Whitehall" dated 1683, at the end of Dorchester Street. (Tomlins, 150–4).

Such old landmarks were often carelessly vandalised at the time when London was rapidly expanding. These had escaped destruction until then probably because of a temporary fashion for archery in the 1780s, when the old jealous guardianship of the butts was revived, with beating of the bounds, removal of obstructions, and marking the rovers. Some that had been broken up were even replaced. (Ib., 153–6, n.)

In 1817 most of the Clothworkers' Company land was let as pasture or hayfields to the dairy farmers Samuel and James Rhodes. The value was enhanced early in the 19th century by two developments in transport: first in 1812 when the New North Road, linking Islington at its eastern border with the City, was built through the eastern fringe of the estate, cutting off a small triangular piece. Secondly, by 1820 the Regent's Canal, a convenient means of industrial carriage, was completed across the south-east of the estate. As late as 1842 Samuel Lewis commented that the new road in spite of saving $\frac{3}{4}$-mile between Highbury Place and Shoreditch, was "little used", but that it had "given a spur to building and houses and streets have been rapidly formed; so that Islington and Hoxton are now nearly united by continuous lines of buildings". (p. 404)

Early in Queen Victoria's reign the demand for building land was intense, but profitable development on the Clothworkers' land was at first hindered because the tenure was copyhold, and leases were limited to 21 years.

The Company made an unsuccessful attempt to enfranchise their land in 1842, and eventually achieved it in 1845 for their original Corporate Estate, and in 1846 for the Packington estate, in consideration of the latter's allowing the Ecclesiastical Commissioners some 4 acres to include a church site on the eastern corner of their land, bounded in part by the new road and by the canal. Now free of restrictions, The Company could begin building.

Their still rural estate was bounded on the SE by the Regent's Canal, on the NE by the New North Road (with the triangular field beyond), on the NW by Frog Lane – continuation of what was to become Prebend Street – and on the West by the site of the future Union Square and Bevan Street. A proposed street layout was established, 80-year building leases were granted, and between 1846 and 1858 the estate was entirely built up.

There were some half-dozen developers, most of whom engaged builders or further sub-leased the properties when built. Chief and best known was the builder of

Arlington and Union Squares, Henry Rydon, of Oakley Crescent off the City Road, who, though he appears to have had no early training as builder or craftsman, not only had the finance and initiative but was a good organiser and entrepreneur. He had come from Somerset and started in business only a few years earlier, as a tailor in Finsbury Circus; now he combined his Clothworkers' Estate activities with developing the neighbouring Wenlock Barn estate in Hackney for the Ecclesiastical Commissioners, and in the 1850s was to go on to the building of Highbury New Park.

Rydon built, or had built for him, about 240 houses on the Clothworkers' estate, and 95 on the part taken by the Ecclesiastical Commissioners. His work was generally of a high standard, and he was honoured by having both a street and a pub named after him, Other builders or sub-contractors, such as Rowland & Evans, Job Palmer, and John Hebb, were men of substance, yet few built more than a handful of contiguous houses here. Rydon, on completion of his part, sold the improved ground rents with first option to the Commissioners (because of "the handsome way in which [they] have always treated me"); and having disposed of his interests in the area, passed on to the Highbury New Park venture.

Building style of the estate

The oddly shaped estate built over some dozen years has the peculiarity of exceptionally wide straight streets, with diagonals marking the awkward angles of its outer boundaries. On the part of the estate lying on the far side of the New North Road, the only feasible layout was not even a square but a triangle (Wilton Square). In spite of broad highways, however, except in Arlington Square and Union Square the Clothworkers' houses are surprisingly small and low-rise. Mostly two-storey with basements, they have disproportionately high parapets, which look better in the streets with stucco mouldings (e.g. St Paul Street) than in those without (e.g. Rector Street); though some of the former have retained the stucco but lost the mouldings (e.g. Canon Street). They are remarkably uniform, not to say monotonous, but (as stipulated in the building agreement) substantial.

Within the simple overall design there is variation of detail according to the different builders: e.g. Coleman Fields (Charles Haswell) has triangular door-pediments and a double string-course at first-floor level.

The houses had to conform with surveyor's specifications, and to be set back at least 5 feet behind open areas, and be provided with railings and Portland stone kerbs. The basements must be at least 8 ft high, ground floor $9\frac{1}{2}$, first floor 9, and the "two pair square storey floors" at least 8. Materials included stock bricks with "cement dressings and cornices, Portland stone steps, sills and copings to fronts, and York stone to the back fronts". The timber must be Scandinavian, not American, the roofs of Duchess-size slate, garden walls 6 ft high of brick; and no manufacturing buildings were allowed in the precincts without consent.

Arlington Square (1849–51) and development of the estate

Rydon built more or less from east to west, starting from New North Road and ending with Arlington Square south side and Union Square east side (December 1851). (The exact orientation of the squares sides is NW, NE, etc., but for the purposes of this account they are referred to as North, East etc.)

Rydon sub-leased to the builders William Catling, John Hill (who shortly went bankrupt) and others, and Catling built half of the W side and Hill most of the E side. Other builders in the Square were Edward Rowland and Thomas Evans. Last to be finished were nos. 27–29 on the S side, in December 1851; the total was 46 houses. In 1854–6 the Ecclesiastical Commissioners built a district church, parsonage and school at the northern tip of the square.

On the canal side, concealing Sturt's Lock, are two pairs of high wooden doors leading to Arlington Wharf and the towpath. (Islington Film Studios operated here, in Poole Street, in the years 1919–49 – actually in Hackney, despite the name.) This side is contiguous with Arlington Avenue, which gives way at no. 44 to square numbering, as nos. 12–21, and resumes beyond the second canal gate at no. 47.

Residents of the square, as of the estate generally, were clerks, compositors, cabinet makers, commercial travellers, servants, shopkeepers, warehousemen – a spectrum of respectable trades and callings but by no means part of Islington's top-ranking or more prosperous society.* By the 1870s there are signs of conversion to workshops for the millinery trade. Indeed, the area east of Essex Road was among the parish's poorer developments, and its mushroom growth early posed social problems. St Mary's vicar, the Rev. Daniel Wilson, wrote at New Year 1856, "Those of you who have not recently visited that locality, can have no conception of the rapid increase of its population . . . A new town, indeed, has risen there." The new area's population was already 6,000, 2,000 of them poor and living in 3rd- and 4th-rate houses.

In 1927, when the first leases expired, there were 1,052 properties, whose management The Company then took over, instituting a street-by-street maintenance programme through an estate office. In 1937 they transferred the Packington estate and its charities to the City Parochial Foundation. During the war most of the Corporate Estate properties were badly damaged by bombing, and many families had to be evacuated. The Company however repaired the surviving houses (49 had been totally destroyed), and in December 1945 sold the old Corporate Estate to the London and Manchester Assurance Co. Ltd. In appearance it survives much as it was, many individual buyers having acquired the freeholds.

*For example, in 1853 no. 11 was a surgeon's, and at nos. 36 and 39 were two schools – "academies" rather – run by the Misses Julia, Rosa and Letitia Sarson, and Messrs William Henry and John Cornelius Tregear.

In 1960 the Packington estate was also sold, to private developers, but Islington Council acquired this in 1963, demolished much of it and rebuilt as Council flats, including half of Union Square (q.v.).

St Philip's Church

Islington's population expansion in the 1850s caused serious overloading in the parish of St Mary's, whose church had space for only 1,500. Neither the three Commissioners' churches built in the 1820s by Barry (including Holy Trinity, Cloudesley Square), nor the vicar's campaign in the 1830s, resulting in three more churches (of which the nearest to this area was St Stephen's, Canonbury Road) could accommodate more than a fraction of the inhabitants. Islington now numbered 17,500 inhabitants and the numbers were still increasing. Because of the new area's poverty, a campaign was launched to raise a subscription to provide a church, on a site reserved from the beginning (see above).

Only three of the subscription committee actually lived on the Clothworkers' estate, and only nine people from the area attended the campaign's initial meeting, which was packed with church officials and inhabitants of Canonbury – particularly Compton Terrace – which suggests heavy pressure from the incumbent. Samuel Lewis, of 19 Compton Terrace, and subsequently his son, the historian of Islington, acted as treasurer. The vicar and his father the former vicar, the Rt Revd Daniel Wilson senior, now Bishop of Calcutta, between them subscribed £300, and numerous other clergy and local dignitaries were on the list.

As often happened, a temporary iron church was erected for use until the new church was completed. Meanwhile on 25 October, 1855 the chancel stone was laid by the Revd Daniel, when coins and a scroll were deposited in a bottle beneath the marble slab inscribed with the event.

The architect of St Philip's Church was A. D. Gough, partner of Roumieu of Milner Square fame, and designer also of St Matthew's Church at the corner of Essex Road and Canonbury Street, which was destroyed in the Second World War. St Philip's, in the then fashionable Kentish rag, was in Norman and Early English style, with at the NW corner a four-stage tower with squat spire and square pinnacled corner turrets. W. W. Begley, writing in *The Builder* in 1946, while allowing that Gough "saddled Islington with some weird examples of church architecture", found St Philip's "romanesque solidity" impressive. (*Builder*, 22 March, 1946, "London's Lost Churches"). The adjoining vicarage naturally also tended to the Gothic, rather than the classical of the houses in the square. A national school was built alongside. *The Ecclesiologist*, which normally disapproved of Gough, so modified its attitude as to allow that this was at least "destitute of the extravagances in which [he] luxuriated in his earlier works" (No. CVII, Dec. 1856, p. 427).

Because of the money shortage there were delays in completion. "For the first time in the annals of Islington, the spectacle will be presented of a church standing with

St Philip's Church, Arlington Square in 1942
demolished in 1954 and replaced by flats

bare walls, in the midst of a dense population, because funds are wanting to complete it." [Vicar's address]. The church, which accommodated 1,100 people, was finally consecrated as St Philip's the Evangelist early in January 1857, and served the district for just under a century.

Its later history is a sad one. At the end of the Second World War the church was in a decaying state, like the square generally, but whereas the square gardens were handed over to Islington Council by the London & Manchester Assurance Company in the late 1940s, and restored and reopened by 1953, the church was closed down, made redundant both by falling population and falling congregation. The parish was merged with another church on the Clothworkers' estate, St James's in Prebend Street nearby.

In 1954 St Philip's was being used as a store for cardboard boxes. After fire destroyed part of the building, permission was given for its removal. Though not in itself a beautiful structure, St Philip's has been poorly succeeded by Arbon Court, which is not even aligned to the square's frontage.

Architecture

Although one of Islington's few squares to be built in uniform style, Arlington Square was never wholly symmetrical, partly because of the odd siting of the church on its north-east corner, and partly because West and East sides are not equal, with seven and ten houses respectively. Like Union Square, its houses are a storey higher than the others on the estate, yet appear low from the width of the central garden (cf. Thornhill Square). The broad streets, entering the square at every corner, contribute to the open effect, so that no terraces link. The south side is continuous with the slightly more elegant Arlington Avenue, separated by the gateways to the canal (q.v.).

The three-floor-and-basement houses are flat-fronted with no doorcase pediments; all features are rectangular, fanlights plain; ground-floor stuccoing — including simulated keystones — is carried to the base of the first-floor windows, which have heavy bracketed heads. The heavy cornice is typical of the estate. A number of rococo style window-guards, of flowing grapevine design, survive on ground and first-floor windows.

No. 1 (E side), a heavy double-fronted villa with two single-bay windows and a large circular door-surround, was formerly St Philip's, now St James's Vicarage. Adjoining this, Arbon Court (1958), a featureless Council cube, replaces the demolished St Philip's Church.

The N side of the square is actually Linton Street. Nos. 35–39, just off the NE corner, is a short, extraordinarily top-heavy terrace of three houses, lopsided from having only one (pedimented) door facing front — the others are in Coleman Fields and St Philip's Way — and crowned with a disproportionate expanse of brick and cornice above its segmental windows, like a heavy brow: possibly built by the plasterer John Palmer, of Wenlock Street, Hoxton, a sub-lessee of Rydon's who had worked closely with him on the earlier Wenlock Barn development. [GLC Report p. 4]

Arundel Square (1850–60)

The most northerly and, except for Edward Square, latest of Islington's Victorian squares illustrates the decadence of the medium left behind by fashion. It was built on land known as Pocock's Fields, originally part of Barnsbury manor.

The Pococks were a Berkshire family from the Newbury area, who moved to Shoreditch adjoining the City during the reign of Queen Anne. One descendant, a coal merchant, traded in the City at St Bride's Wharf; another, Richard, acquired land north of the village of Islington including the 14 acres of grassland (1826) on which Arundel Square was later to be built. His son Samuel in 1841 owned all open land between the Back Road and the new Pentonville Prison (VCH p. 68).

At this time the south side of Bride Street (named after the coal wharf) was given over to gardens, which in 1848 were sought for building purposes. Building accordingly began in 1850, but piecemeal, row by row. The east side of the square, nos. 1–17, was completed by 1852, the north side, nos. 18–37, in 1855–60. The west side, though numbered with the square, is really part of Westbourne Road (late 1850s–1860), and the intention to complete a full square failed apparently because money gave out: instead of a south side, the inhabitants got a railway, running through a deep cutting between the square and the backs of Offord Road houses.

Given the odd layout, no consistent numbering was possible, but the method adopted was fairly illogical. The east side numbers run N–S, nos. 1–6 extending north of the square limits, and nos. 7–16 are in the square proper, ending at Arundel Place, the link with Offord Road. Numbering is then picked up on the north side, E–W (18–37), but west side runs S–N (38–48), interrupting Westbourne Road, then continuing as the 'Road' as far as the former St Clement's Church.

On the death of a former owner in 1957, dispute over the disposal of 14 of the north side properties ended with their sale to Circle 33 Housing Trust, which converted the houses to 60 flats, internally modernised. In 1970 the square was among the first properties in Islington Borough to be designated part of a conservation area under the 1967 Act. Many houses have been converted to flats and maisonettes.

Architecture
The square – actually a parallelogram by the alignment of the W side – provides typical Islington contrasts. The E side, as an extension of Arundel Place, is an orthodox early/mid-Victorian terrace of tall houses, for years shabby, now restored by the Council. Their 'Before' and 'After' contrast makes a good illustration of how

Arundel Square in the 1960s
The over-crowded north side (1855-60) is the most elaborate in this
incomplete square

such terraces respond to changed conditions, and how, except for war damage, Islington survived largely untouched until rehabilitation in recent years. Nos. 1–15 form a complete terrace with balancing end-features and quoins, and circular-headed windows in the central houses. Nos. 16–17 were to disappear in 1867 with the building of the North London Railway. No. 16 was rebuilt 1984, outwith the terrace proper (vide the quoins of no. 15), but in keeping.

The west side (architecturally part of Westbourne Road) is undistinguished late 1850s, stuccoed ground floors, segmental window- and door-heads and vermicular keystones. The end house to the south (no. 38) boasts a more elaborate porch with floral carvings and stubby half-columns. An early photograph shows a diaper brick pattern on the end wall, with the date 1860, which has now disappeared. At nos. 53/54, beyond the square's limits, is a pend or entry crowned by a flamboyant lion mask in stucco.

The north side offers the greatest interest, with echoes of Italianate South Kensington or Bayswater, e.g. Powis Square. Its houses, four floors and basement, are exceptionally tall for Islington of that date, and the skinny porches have slim Ionic columns, without entasis. These are double porticoes; originally they were designed for triple columns, the centre one shared between two houses (possibly a money-saving device), but only the westernmost one remains (nos. 36/37). In fact a postcard view of *c.* 1906 shows them with only two columns. Continuous 'features' from top to bottom emphasise the verticality, such as the stucco aprons crammed one above the other. Ground floors are stuccoed, with round window-heads and fanlights, and a profusion of vermicular rustication – quoins, keystones to the windows, and shell brackets between houses, though a number have been lost, as have several of the porch column capitals. The close-set panes in the first-floor windows also emphasise the narrowness of the houses, in a style as it were too grand for their width. Thistle-motif balconies are supported by stone brackets. Above the 2nd-floor cornice the façade is plain. The east end of this range is windowless, broken up with blind window mouldings on three levels, and panels at ground level, as are the corner houses of adjoining Ellington Street.

St Clement's Church (Gilbert Scott, 1863–5)
Lofty but towerless, this was a district church, preceded, as so often, by a temporary iron structure in the square. At £7,000 it was rather grand and expensive, paid for by the patron George Cubitt, MP, 1st Lord Ashcombe, as a proprietory chapel for the modest neighbourhood. On this side it is almost swallowed by the adjoining houses, revealing only the triple lancets of its E end, with glass by Clayton and Bell. The West entrance has three brick portals in its tall façade, and highly pitched roof with buttresses and bell-cote. Like most local churches it was built by Dove Brothers. In 1966 the organ of St Thomas's Church, Regent Street, with more than 1,200 pipes, was installed here.

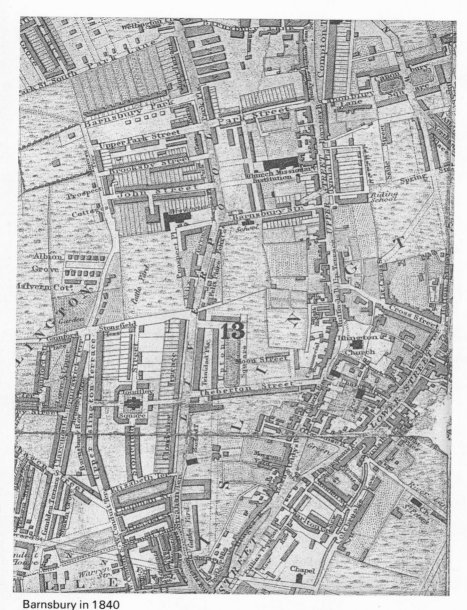

Barnsbury in 1840
Detail from Ruff's map: site of Barnsbury Square (field west of Barnsbury
Park); Cloudesley Square; beginnings of Milner-Gibson estate (Gibson
Square as "Upton Square"); site of Lonsdale Square ("cattle yard"); Malvern
Terrace shown as Malvern Cottages in two parts, with south part of Compton
Terrace; Colebrooke Row/Duncan Terrace near bottom right

In 1968 it was declared redundant, and for some years used by a Greek Orthodox congregation; now deconsecrated and converted as flats. In 1976 the parish was united with St David's, Westbourne Road.

Gardens
Originally these were maintained by Pocock's trustees as open space, and from 1863 by a residents' committee. By the 1950s the gardens were run-down and had reverted to waste ground; in 1957 the Council converted them to a public park and playground, which later developed its own playgroup and local festival.

Inhabitants
No famous names are recorded as living in Arundel Square — perhaps because in Edwardian times at least the smarter north side supposedly housed the kept mistresses of City men. In the 1870s it had been distinctly respectable, with a couple of clergymen and an architect, and at no. 59 [sic] a ladies' school kept by the Misses Ann and Emma Sarah Walls.

Barnsbury Square (1827; 1835–44)

Few spots in Islington can have been looked on as more historic than the moated enclosure on the site of Barnsbury Square. Reed Moat Field, on the flat hill-top north of Pentonville and the White Conduit, was the survival of a mediaeval farm once belonging to Barnsbury Manor, but throughout a large part of the 18th century topographers and historians had identified both Highbury's and Barnsbury's earthworks as ancient encampments, the former of Britons, perhaps Romans, maybe Danes . . . the latter, however, seemed incontrovertibly Roman.

In 1756, in *England's Gazetteer*, Stephen Whatley started a hare which was to be pursued even to recent years: that the enclosure, "the third field beyond the White Conduit", with remains of trenches and a kind of rampart, was "supposed to have been a Roman camp, made use of by Suetonius Paulinus after his retreat . . . from London", before he went on to confront and rout Queen Boadicea — traditionally held to be at Battle Bridge, near present-day King's Cross.

Later writers repeated and embroidered the supposition, among them Lysons in his *Environs* (1792–1811), and *The Ambulator*, a topical account of London frequently revised and updated – and of course Islington historians, from Nelson onwards.

The evocative Reed Moat Field was much illustrated by local water-colourists. The open ridge commanded views over the vale of Maiden Lane, including unsavoury kilns and 'nuisance industries', and from 1826, the new Chalk Road, towards the green slopes of Highgate and Hampstead. Dent's Survey of 1805/6 outlines the 'camp', without identifying it, at one end of an irregularly shaped field

Reed Moat Field, Barnsbury
From a 19th-century water-colour by C. H. Matthews

(plot 105), which he names "Gravelpit field, Workhouse field and Moat field, now in one". The Workhouse was indeed a stone's-throw away to the south-east, while a little way south of that was almost the only house in the vicinity, Thomas Albion Oldfield's.

Nelson (1811,p. 65) refers in passing to the "camp, with its evidently Roman" Praetorium, defensive rampart and sedgy fosse, during an exhaustive account of the campaign of Suetonius and the supposed local battle. (It is now established to have been miles away, in the Midlands.) Some 15 years later a correspondent "T.A.", or Thomas Allen, in William Hone's *Everyday Book*, takes the myth further by mentioning arrowheads and tiles dug up by road-mending labourers in 1825. (II. 1566, lifted without acknowledgement by Lewis in 1842, p. 335). Unfortunately this promising evidence was dug back again, to become foundations of the unidentified road (Caledonian? Hemingford?). Worse, the moat was drained in 1826 and the site subsequently excavated for building materials.

Cromwell in 1835 illustrates the 'camp' in its state of about 30 years earlier, lifting Nelson's account with little change (pp. 390–1), and Lewis in turn plagiarises Cromwell: enclosure about 200 feet square, fosse 20–30 feet wide and 12 feet deep, full of water and overgrown with sedge. According to Cromwell, in about 1820 the surroundings had been "in great degree broken up by digging for brick-clay and gravel", though the grassy 'Praetorium' was still visible and the long western rampart survived, probably little changed over the centuries. "On fine summer evenings it usually swarms with children at their various pastimes . . . "(p. 396).

First to throw cold water on the attractive myth was Thomas Tomlins in his *Perambulation of Islington* (1858). Having investigated the dubious tales of Roman finds he notes that when Mountfort House was built on the moated site, drained in 1826, nothing relevant was excavated. He dismisses Hone's arrowhead finder of 1825 as "an illiterate labourer", and the objects that turned up on the house site as probably "some few of the old halfpence, &c. commonly found in sewers", which "cunning labourers" often passed off as Roman. In short, "the hackneyed terms, *Praetorium*, and *Fosse*" were recklessly applied, and the "vestige" of the site could as credibly be given a Danish origin, or Saxon, or even "much later . . . a manorial residence since the Conquest" (p. 174 & n.). [See also *The Gentleman's Magazine*, XVIII NS, 144]

So much for the romance of the site.

Although Tomlins was at last on the right track, a picturesque theory is hard to kill. Even in the 1970s when the mediaeval origin was accepted, Islington Council erected a plaque on Mountfort House recording it as site of a "Roman camp". It has recently been removed.

Later building on all sides obliterated all signs of the enclosure, and unfortunately Barnsbury Square's garden, which might have been supposed a natural means of preserving the old earthwork, is not on the site at all. Our ancestors, especially builders, were not squeamish about flattening historic relics, and first it was relegated to the extensive grounds behind Mountfort House, where indeed it remained visible, for Sir Johnston Forbes-Robertson, reminiscing in 1925 about his childhood there, recalls "a considerable dip or trench" in the garden (and goes on to repeat the popular Roman camp story). Any hope of recovering archaeological evidence vanished in the 1930s when a factory extension was built on to the rear of the house.

Pond Field and early leases

The history of Barnsbury Square and its gardens is among the most tortuous in Islington, and much remains to be unravelled. Intensive investigation of the Middlesex Deeds Register and Islington Rate Books, supplemented by contemporary comments, proves not completely illuminating, but the facts so far as can be deduced are as follows.

Although Dent's 1805/6 survey describes the area of the famous earthwork (as we have seen) as a conflation of "Gravelpit Field, Workhouse Field and Moat Field", and owned by Nathaniel Bishop, Esq., the name used in all leases and agreements is Pond Field. The earliest of these shows that in 1810 Mr Bishop, then living in the village of Paddington, leased Pond Field and land east of it as far as the Back Road, for 99 years to Robert Clarke younger, Esq., of Oundle in Northamptonshire. This was apparently part of a larger transaction, and 20 years later was confirmed by a new lease of December 1830, presumably with a view to building. (MDR 1831/2/162)

Between Pond Field and the Back Road the area demised was bounded by the south side of Barnsbury Park and north side of Brooksby Street — whose name commemorates the Leicestershire village where Robert Clarke had formerly lived. Some building had already started in the 1820s and new roads had been laid out: Upper Park Street (now Bewdley Street) running east and west, and Minerva Road or Street (later part of Thornhill Road) running N/S, separating Pond Field from the other property. On part of this Minerva Terrace (62–82 Thornhill Road) had been begun in 1827, apparently by Louis England (see Cloudesley and Gibson Squares), but most of the site was undeveloped, and on Pond Field in particular the 1830 agreement states that "no building hath been at present erected".

Development was very much in the air, however, and another builder, Thomas Harding Bilham, living in John Street (Lofting Road) had already run up four houses on the south side of Upper Park Street and appears to have completed nos. 32–34 Brooksby Street, north side (Ib.) That England built Minerva Terrace where he did may have been mere coincidence, and although it may be regarded as part of Barnsbury Square, it was never integrated into it and the square developed in a totally unorthodox way.

Robert Clarke, who evidently had no active interest in building, in April 1832 made over the reversion of the lease to someone who did, and who was also speculating in land in St Pancras: Mr John Huskisson, a chemist living in Swinton Street off the Gray's Inn Road. Huskisson in turn leased the land east of Pond Field to Thomas Bilham, who proceeded to erect houses on the south side of Barnsbury Park, the north side of Upper Park Street, and — finally — in Barnsbury Square. To Bilham, it appears, we can ascribe the distinctive type of Barnsbury villa or semi-detached, characterised by segmental arches over the main windows, adorned with a wreath. This motif appears in houses on the side of Barnsbury Park specified as built by Bilham in leases of (for example), 1833 and 1835, the 5th and 6th, 7th and 8th, 9th and 10th houses from the Liverpool Road (leases, Huskisson to Bilham, MDR 1833/8/270 & 271, 1835/7/504).

Huskisson continued to lease out the land, and in April 1834 comes the first reference to Barnsbury Square and its chief developer. This was Thomas Whowell, gentleman, then living in Prospect Cottages just north of the new "Minerva Road". Whowell acquired all the part of Pond Field west of "a newly intended Square called or then intended to be called Barnesbury Square", including the ancient moated site; and here by 1835 he built, or caused to be built, the substantial small mansion called Mountfort House. Cromwell, writing soon after, sees little good in it:

"Streets, and other lines of buildings, detached cottages, gardens, &c. are now in almost immediate contiguity . . . and the praetorium itself is occupied by a large house, with its grounds, at the time of this writing finishing, and 'to let '. The carriage drive round the house is made to fall into the north and west channels of the fosse, which, on the east side, is quite filled up, to afford access to the principal front, and on the south is excluded by the garden wall, and has there become a stagnant ditch." (p. 396)

He gives a picture of destruction of the hilltop fields, and Barnsbury's descent to mere suburb.

"Minerva Terrace, looking due west over the remains of this ancient relic, is just completed ... An open road (though not as yet a carriage thoroughfare) [i.e. Minerva Road] runs from the west end of Barnsbury Park, before these houses, to Oldfield's Dairy and the Albion Cricket-ground." (p. 397)

He foresees that more building will soon shut out the rural views: for example Prospect Cottages – Whowell's own base (later 38–60 Thornhill Road, demolished in the 1970s) – "have lost their prospect", though some owners have temporarily staved off building of further new "cottages" by "cultivating the land in front as pleasure ground".

Thomas Oldfield's Dairy and tea gardens, in the same family for generations, were no longer in the country. His cricket-field where the Albion club had played for some quarter of a century, as modest successor to the earlier aristocratic players who had moved on to become the Marylebone Cricket Club at Lord's, saw its last match in the summer of 1834, and they themselves left for a still unthreatened site near Copenhagen House. Minerva Street, still evidently unpaved, linked with "the broad footpath before the Albion", and south of this with "two spacious carriage roads", namely Cloudesley and Barnsbury Roads, both then a series of terraces built in the 1820s. Other new Barnsbury terraces were of meaner quality. All this belonged to Holy Trinity district, a new creation with the building of the Cloudesley estate, and in 1841 its population was still a mere 7,322, and the number of houses built so far was computed at 1,110, with 18 uninhabited and 86 still building (Lewis, p. 334).

Opposite Minerva Terrace, briefly mentioned by Cromwell, there was shortly built, as Tomlins notes in 1858, "the enclosure of Barnsbury Square, which together with the detached houses and gardens on the south, west and north sides thereof (called the Mountfort Estate) occupy the grounds of what was the Reedmoat Field" (p. 172).

Mountfort House first appears in Rate Books only by Christmas 1836. With its spacious front and shell mouldings it was considerably more elaborate than other houses building in Islington, and Whowell may have had aspirations to grandeur, for not only did he continue to build in a fashion unorthodox for the area, but by the 1840s he is styling himself "Esquire" – that is to say, a 'real' gentleman as opposed to

Mountfort House, Barnsbury Square in 1953
showing industrial chimney at rear, since demolished

merely a person of independent means — and was calling the area, as Tomlins later does, "the Mountfort Estate".

Barnsbury, unique among Islington's squares in not evolving as terraces, consists of single and paired villas bordering the central space. Further, its west side as laid out by Whowell is eccentric, with loop-like excrescences north and south of Mountfort House. On both of these Whowell seems originally to have proposed villas ranged crescent-style round smaller spaces, as indicated on plan in a lease of February 1837 (MDR 1837/1/566); he eventually settled for a short terrace on the south, by linking two rather grander detached houses (nos. 1 and 4 Mountfort Terrace) with two slightly smaller (nos. 2 and 3), while leaving the still larger villa, now no. 7 Barnsbury Square, free-standing to the east. The sites for nos. 2 and 3 of the terrace Whowell leased in September 1843 to another builder, William Grimman, of 7 Camden Street, with the houses "now being erected", which suggests that Grimman actually built these two. (MDR 1843/8/531—2) The large villa, with one foot on the south side of the square and another as it were in Mountfort Terrace, was at first named "Suetonius Lodge", soon mercifully transformed to "West Lodge".

Mountfort Crescent, begun in 1841, was intended for five houses — the eastern-most appears to have been planned as a double-fronted single. In the event the two pairs of charming bow-fronted semi-detacheds were built, while the fifth house was completed in 1844 with its bows facing inwards, so that the crescent-effect is not fully brought off.

The leases suggest that north and south sides of the square were built in 1837. At least part of the south side, four pairs of simple semi-detached villas, was let to William Slark, Esq. On the north the sites of the first and second houses from Minerva Road (i.e. Thornhill Road) were leased to Benjamin Green, builder, of Morgan's Place, Liverpool Road. These houses are built in the 'Barnsbury' style, but Thomas Bilham died in July 1836,* and his widow Frances began disposing of all his leasehold property; so that perhaps Green built these houses in Bilham's style, or borrowing some of his favourite motifs. The Rate Book for 1837/8 enters "2 houses in here" as an addition, four are recorded, empty, in 1838 and all are occupied by 1839.

The foregoing seems the simplest and most likely interpretation of the known facts, as no direct account is given of the building of any of these houses, and those on the south side are not mentioned at all, merely outlined on a plan of 1844 (MDR 1844/4/162), and appearing fully-fledged in Rate Books and Directories.

Whowell seems not to have intended Mountfort House for himself, and it was subdivided into two and let to two clergymen, the Rev. John Jackson and the Rev. Henry Beamish, who from 1840/41 was replaced by the Rev. Henry Hamilton —

*Bilham, who was 50, was buried at St Mary's parish church on 26 July, 1836. Nathaniel Bishop, progenitor of all this building activity, is also recorded in the parish register as being buried at St Mary's, on 27 April, 1836. He was aged 75 and was then living in Hammersmith. (GL Rec. Off., P83/St Mary, microfilm X85/107)

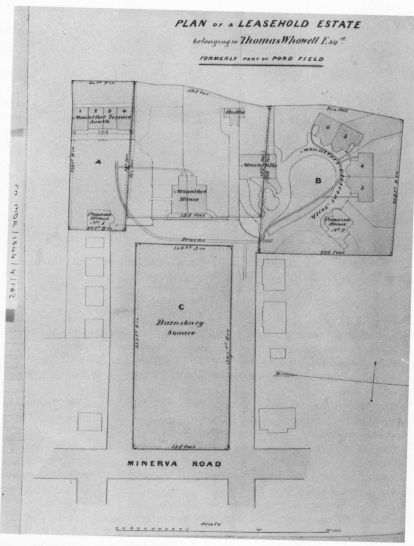

Plan of Barnsbury Square in 1844
Layout of the former Pond Field, with Mountfort House, Crescent and
Terrace, and sites of proposed houses. (GLRO plan MDR 1844/4/162)

Mountfort Crescent in 1939

Headmaster and assistant at the Islington Proprietary School (see Milner Square). At first Whowell seems to have occupied the single house in Mountfort Crescent, which subsequently became the vicarage for Holy Trinity Church and later for St Andrew's; he then moved (he was always moving) to "Mount Villa", a modest house between Mountfort House and the Crescent. Some years earlier he had started to make over the property to others. In 1844 it was to William Charles Rickman, J. F. Tourle, and the Rev. Joseph Frederick Hone, of Tirley in Gloucestershire, who appears to have become his son-in-law.

Whowell lived in the square until 1847, after which we lose sight of him. He may have died then or soon after; he was certainly dead by 1856, for his widow Catherine started legal proceedings against Rickman, Hone and Tourle over the land ownership. (GL Rec. Off. Acc. 2306/1.2)

The complexities of the square's leases and mortgages, however, would form a weighty subject of research, as Thomas Bilham's widow disposed of his property leased from Huskisson, and Whowell was no sooner building than he was mortgaging and demising his houses. For the purposes of this account we may ignore these changes and move on to later episodes in the square's unfortunate history, which are even more convoluted.

Later history

At first there was a long period of palmy days, especially during the time when the Forbes-Robertson family lived at Mountfort House, which as the celebrated Shakespearean actor Sir Johnston Forbes-Robertson recalled in 1925, was from 1859–74 (see p. 24). House and garden were both grand. Sir Johnston revealed that in two rooms, including his father's library opening on to the garden, were pilasters that had been removed from Carlton House when it was demolished in 1826. More famously, other columns were re-used for the portico of the National Gallery.

Besides the famous 'Roman' earthwork, which was in a "deep vale", where were also a coach-house and stable — though the family never managed to keep either carriage or horses — there were "many fine trees and laburnum and lilac", and a mulberry tree.

The square always housed a large proportion of clergy, and the odd architect and portrait painter. In the 1880s and 1890s a couple of private schools appear, and from 1896 Mountfort House was run as a Home for Destitute Boys by Mrs Margaret Watts Hughes, and from 1910 by the Rev. Charles Spencer.

But as usual the rot set in. Barnsbury Square's layout, which precluded a symmetrical appearance for building, proved its misfortune. While the east side may be said to be completed by Minerva Terrace, the west was dictated by the central placing of Mountfort House, pushing out further building to the corners. North and south sides were curtailed by the long back gardens of Thornhill Road's corner houses which extended a good part of their length. As the century progressed, and Barnsbury's prosperity declined, these gardens and the back garden of Mountfort House became prey to industrial development, and no latter-day face-lift is likely to reverse the effects of this.

In 1914 Mountfort House was taken by Henry Gibbs, identified in the 1923 Directory as "silk dyer", and the house was converted to industrial use. In 1944 the firm is named as the English and French Dyeing Company Ltd. Meanwhile in 1935 Mica & Micanite Supplies, of 1, Offord Street, acquired the whole garden ground north of and behind the house, which was then virtually encased in a huge factory building, Mica House (architects Chamberlain & Willows), with long horizontals and continuous windows, characteristic of the period but incongruous in this setting. North of Mountfort House a single-storey workshop, with asbestos-corrugated roof, extended the length of the garden, with a tall industrial chimney at the rear. The spacious grounds and remains of the "rampart " were thus obliterated.

So things remained (though the chimney was dismantled in the 1970s), until in the 1980s various changes of ownership took place, and after a period lying empty Mountfort House has been restored and converted to office suites (1990); in 1992 plans were in hand for reversion of the secondary, south-facing house to a private dwelling, and for Mica House to be transformed into apartments and studios. The north-side workshop is now used for furniture manufacture. (see p. 34).

The south side of the square has also suffered from industrial infiltration, with the turn-of-the-century rebuilding of 35 Thornhill Road and addition of workshops to its back garden, encroaching on the side of the square. There was Victorian infilling, and no. 6 rebuilt handsomely enough in the later 19th century, is now incongruously tacked in to its modest neighbour with monstrous effect.

On the north side, two of the original paired villas survive; the western pair was destroyed in the war, and a row of six linked low-rise houses running south to north was fitted into the site of the two houses and their back gardens. The other houses have all survived reasonably well.

The fight for the gardens

The central gardens of Barnsbury Square contain an acre of ground, roughly rectangular, 134 feet on east and west, 299 on the north, 308 on the south. The surrounding estate eventually comprised 29 houses, whose leases had always included the right to the 'soil' of the square, and covenants ensuring that the gardens were maintained as ornamental pleasure grounds for the residents. Until, that is, the original 99-year lease expired, which would be in 1909.

In 1889 the Metropolitan Public Gardens Association purchased the lease of the gardens, laid them out as a park, and in 1891 transferred them to Islington Vestry, for whom the Duke and Duchess of Westminster ceremonially opened them.

For long-term protection, however, it would be necessary to buy up the reversionary interests. From the end of 1905 the 29 freeholders elected a committee through whom they negotiated with the Town Hall, offering to settle for half the land valuation of £12,000 provided the gardens could be maintained for the public. The MPGA also urged the Council to purchase: "It would be a calamity if this fine London Square were to be covered with buildings"; but having taken the initiative 20 years earlier, the Association now considered the ball to be in the Council's court.

One of many complications was the discovery that in the 1880s Mr Zambra, of the shoe firm Negretti & Zambra, had purchased the whole estate of 29 houses, with the right to the 'soil' of the square, and had split it into individual freeholds, which meant obtaining the consent of 29 owners – or 30, since Mountfort House was now treated as two – before any agreement could be concluded. Certain owners stood out, or could not be found, lawyers were consulted, recriminations and misinterpretations were rife. The land value was contested and obscure freeholders were sought out. Donaldson's, a firm of estate agents acting for Benjamin Levi, who owned nos. 2–5 Barnsbury Square and thus had four shares, surveyed the estate and urged that it "would form an admirable building site, being an island plot, surrounded on all sides by roads made, channelled and sewered, in the heart of a populous neighbourhood, within a short distance of the City of London and with every facility of access". A familiar argument.

Neither the MPGA nor the LCC wished to be involved. Arguments became pettier, extending to whether the gardener's hut and the fountain were fixtures, or 'portables' which might be removed from the garden.

Convoluted reference was made to the original lease and the subsequent complex underleases and agreements, and no less a person than Robert Clarke, Esq., the original lessor of 1810 and 1830, was addressed in the Schedule. It was claimed that the Bishop family, who had first started these transactions, had sold all the ground rents in about 1900.

Lawyers established that all conveyances to the owners contained a covenant that the square must not be built on. They urged that it would be wrong to drive local children from their playground into the street — especially as traffic had "become so largely a Motor traffic".

As the wrangle continued, with the freeholders making more resolutions, the date of expiry of the leases passed without agreement made. In 1911 it was established that one share had been conveyed to the Council in 1894 — two, in fact, since it represented Mountfort House, causing another subject for disagreement. It was next discovered that sale of a house did not convey a *share* to the buyer, but that the share remained vested in the previous owner. At a public meeting in 1912 an attempt was made to convey the gardens to the Council under the Act for preserving London's squares of 1906; but since no one could agree on anything, the lease had to be surrendered.

After these years of hurly-burly, for 20 years the gardens were now left to become derelict.

Not entirely, though. Tennis had these days become all the rage, and by degrees the gardens were taken over by tennis clubs, the ground was levelled to make courts, and embankments were raised over the lawns. But gradually the railings were broken down, and the mature trees damaged.

In 1931 the square was included in Part I of the Schedule to the London Squares Preservation Act, which at least protected it from being built on. After many complaints to the LCC and the Borough Council, at last in 1932 the two bodies discussed maintenance. Still there was the obstacle of the need to secure all the occupiers' agreement, so that a proposal to vest the gardens in a residents' committee, under an old Act of 1863, came to nothing; but in 1933 22 of the 29 freeholders signed a petition praying the LCC to vest the gardens in the Council, under a clause providing for private gardens to be taken in charge when local owners neglected or refused.

This proposal was actually accepted, and that June the gardens were at last transferred to the Borough. The MPGA provided financial support, and on 11 January, 1934, restored and restocked, the square gardens were officially opened by the Mayor. Formerly (noted the *Islington Gazette*), "in a fair way to becoming derelict", they now had "neat lawns and paths, a rockery, running across the length of the upper lawn, a fountain, newly repaired, and teak seats".

This marked the climax of success after an all but disastrous delay, caused by the freeholders' disagreements — and, to be fair, surely no square had had such a legally complex ownership history. But the gardens were now saved from the developers, and have since been excellently maintained by the Council.

Architecture
Most houses are finished overall with stucco, and bows proliferate — in the Crescent throughout, and in no. 13, formerly West Villa, an unusual feature in Islington except (for example) in Barossa Place (see Annett's Crescent) and the rear of Highbury Terrace.

The square is dominated by the 5-bay Mountfort House on the west side, three storeys and basement, front door approached by steps, channelled stucco ground floor with windows in plain arches. First-floor windows have arches with shell moulding, and the low top-floor windows, which interestingly are sliding casements, are placed close under the eaves, between consoles. The mansion-like appearance is deceptive, for the two southern bays belong to its subsidiary house, entered separately on the south front. Apart from the second front door no sign of this division appears on the exterior, and the houses were skilfully designed as two dwellings, apparently from the beginning. One oddity is the top floor's sliding casements, not unlike weavers' or craftsmen's workshop windows. Insertion of metal windows has seriously modified the south side in adapting to industrial and office use, but in 1992 there were plans to replace these and match them to the Barnsbury Square front.

No internal features remain except some cornices and doors, fireplaces and mouldings having been stripped out to leave bland office-wall surfaces, and the Carlton House columns long ago disappeared. The large accretion of Mica House almost enwraps the original building, overlapping on the south and covering the whole garden on the west and side garden to the north. In its own terms it is a successful building, whose large windows will lend themselves well to flatted conversion. On the low north-side workshop, a tiled roof has now replaced the corrugated asbestos.

The picturesque Mountfort Crescent consists of two low paired villas with steep roofs, porticoes, tripartite windows and large bows — a Leamingtonesque effect; while no. 20, intended also for two bows, at the side, has had one replaced by a later Victorian bay. The side facing the square has tripartite windows like no. 13.

Set back between the Crescent and Mountfort House, the modest no. 17 (Mount Villa, later called Hebron), in widely-channelled stucco, has a doll's-house look, with small gabled entrance block and window in an arch above, and flanking windows under segmental hoods.

Mountfort Terrace: Italianate, 3 floors and basement, with balustrades instead of area railings; all features rectangular; the two larger, outer houses 3-bay, well advanced, pavilion-style; the inner houses two-bay. A broad cornice below the top-floor windows; elaborately designed balconies (nos. 1,4) and window-guards

"Hebron", no. 17 Barnsbury Square in 1976, before restoration

(nos. 2 and 3). The north side, undisguised brick, is completely blank except for a thermal window at the top above a broad band (and a later small closet window).

The massive no. 13, 3 storeys and basement, has a bow on the inner (west) side with excessively thin cast-iron column supports. Features rectangular; tripartite windows flank the front door, a grander version above framed by entablatures, and low top windows; dentil frieze and wide cornice, parapet. Above the cill band is a feature like a row of small column bases.

No. 12 is a small late Victorian, villa-style cottage, two storeys and basement, with a canted bay, The original south side houses are nos. 6/7, 8/9, 10/11, paired Barnsbury semi's, attractively modest in brick (no. 9 has been stuccoed), plain except for cill bands between floors. Some have been linked by small extensions. No. 6, however has been refaced, c. 1860s and raised by two storeys to an inordinate height, stuccoed overall, channelled on the ground floor, and with a shallow porch (restored 1992). Nos. 4/5 are an 1890s brick insertion, plaster detail on bays, tall parapet with brackets giving an almost castellated effect. The rest of this side is ?1920s industrial, built out over the former back garden of the rebuilt 35 Thornhill Road.

Opposite, a single pair of the more elaborate Barnsbury-type semi survives in nos. 27 and 28, 3 storeys and basement with low extensions on either side. The main windows are framed in segmental arches containing wreaths, and the entrance bay is set back and stuccoed; no. 28 (all stuccoed) has a pretty, flowery cast-iron Victorian porch whose richness has been described by one observer as "almost Australian". nos. 25/26, destroyed in the war, have been replaced by a neat mews-style development of low, unobtrusive houses in stock brick, c. 1960.

Minerva Terrace (62–82 Thornhill Road) is in standard terrace style, in rhythm 4-3-4, with centre and end houses very slightly advanced. Channelled stucco ground floor with windows circular-headed, cill bands immediately below upper floor windows. The three central houses (70–74) distinguished with first-floor windows in heavier surrounds – as are no. 76's, partly lost – and with a shallow top moulding and parapet. Several houses have had modern attics added. Fanlights plain 'umbrella' style; plain guard-rails, bowing out near the base. The terrace runs from Brooksby to Bewdley Street, with side entrances to the end houses.

Inhabitants

By far the best-known inhabitants of Barnsbury Square were the Forbes-Robertson family at Mountfort House, from 1859–74. John, the father, a successful journalist and art critic, came from Aberdeen, and all his family of 11 were born in the house except Johnston, who was six when they moved in. Johnston was educated locally at a school run by a German (not identified), and later at the Charterhouse. He studied art at the Royal Academy, but soon needing to earn a living went on the stage. He contributed to a long theatrical tradition by studying with Phelps (See Canonbury Square), who had played under Macready, who himself had studied under Sarah Siddons.

Among the numerous visitors to Mountfort House at this time were painters, poets and novelists: Swinburne, Dante Gabriel Rossetti, the Madox Browns, William Morris, Alma-Tadema and George Macdonald, besides other celebrities less remembered to-day. In 1874 the family moved to Bloomsbury. (See Forbes-Robertson's autobiography, *A Player in Five Reigns*, London, 1925, ch.1)

No other famous people seem at that time to have lived in the square, though there was always a high proportion of clergy, and at one time an architect, John Carr McLellan (1883–8), at 3 Mountfort Crescent and at 4 Mountfort Terrace a portrait painter, Frederick Ullman (1886–8).

In Minerva Terrace's early days one inhabitant, from 1828–30, had a name to delight fashionable novel readers of the time – Miss Greciana Casey.

Canonbury Square (1805–9, 1821–30, 1954)
(See also Compton Terrace)

Historical Background

The long rectangle of Canonbury Square was built on what had been part of the old manor of Canons Burh, a dwelling-place of the Canons of St Bartholomew's,

Smithfield, on farm-land passed to them by Ralph de Berners in 1373. Their early house was replaced or embellished by Prior Bolton (c. 1510–30) as a courtyard mansion, open on its west side.

When King Henry VIII confiscated St Bartholomew's Priory in 1539 Prior Bolton's successor, Robert Fuller, was obliged to surrender the manor. The King presented it to Thomas Cromwell, but like many properties granted in those precarious times it reverted to the Crown on its recipient's disgrace, and was later leased to several of the nobility in turn. After 1570 the lessee was the rich John Spencer, Alderman and later knight and Lord Mayor of London, who lived in the City in the grand Crosby Hall. During the last decades of Queen Elizabeth I's reign he rebuilt and beautified his country acquisition at Canonbury. Much of the surviving manorial building is by Spencer, though the famous tower with its strange square central newel stair predates him.

Elizabeth Spencer, Sir John's daughter, eloped with the young Lord Compton, supposedly lowered in a basket from a tower window to her lover disguised as a baker's boy. She was disinherited by her angry father, but reconciled through the Queen's intervention, and her husband, who became the first Earl of Northampton, inherited the Spencer property. The large estate, intact until the middle of this century, lay alongside the populous village of Islington, between the Upper and Lower Streets; its eastern boundary was Hopping Lane (now St Paul's Road), and from the early 17th century the southern verge was the New River.

In 1616 the manor was leased by Sir Francis Bacon, and later by Lord Coventry. After the 1660s the Northampton family ceased altogether to live there, and in the 18th century it was let out as summer lodgings to gentlemen seeking a rural retreat close to London. Many of these, like the Templar Oliver Goldsmith, used to walk up from the City across the fields. The top of the tower commanded a fine country view as well as a distant vista of London.

Bucolic peace remained unshattered until in 1767 Spencer Compton, the 8th Earl, let the then untenanted Canonbury House, outbuildings, and adjoining grounds including the large pond to John Dawes, a City broker, for 61 years at £40 a year. Dawes demolished the south range and on its site built five 'messuages' forming Canonbury Place, which in 1771 he leased from Lord Northampton, and lived in one of them until he turned his attention to Highbury Fields, another country setting, where he initiated the building of a row of similarly sophisticated houses.

Bowling greens and pleasure gardens surrounded Canonbury House and its new terrace, notably at a tavern opposite the tower on the site of the old stables. Part of the land was held by the dairy farmer, Richard Laycock. At some unspecified date, probably in the 1790s, the handsome small mansion for which no records survive was built adjoining the tower, and which has also confusingly come to be known as Canonbury House, partly filling the west side of the old manor house court. Otherwise, rural tranquillity still prevailed until after the turn of the new century.

Canonbury Square

The history of the square begins in April 1803, when the 9th Earl* signed a building agreement with Henry Leroux of Stoke Newington, a gentleman presumably of Huguenot descent, for a 99-year lease of a large plot. It was bounded in part by Hopping Lane, and by the continuation of the turning near the end of Upper Street already called Canonbury Lane, opposite one of Laycock's vast dairy farms. The price ranged from 5 and 6 shillings to £10 per acre, and within 7 years Leroux had to build on "the whole range of the fronts next the Upper Street of Islington, and Canonbury Lane aforesaid, with good and substantial brick messuages or tenements", at least 2nd-rate on the west, and at least 3rd-rate on the south, attached or "detached regularly", making at least 20 houses each on the west and south fronts. The cost, including the necessary "outhouses and conveniences", was to be at least £25,000. Any bricks made from earth dug on the site should net the Earl 9d per 1000. Leroux was prohibited from allowing any nuisance industries such as "Catgut Spinner . . . Cat Skinner . . . or Boiler of Horse-flesh".

The logical place to start building was the high-road site, so it was Compton Terrace on which Leroux first embarked, in the form of a chapel (Union Chapel) flanked by two pairs of houses. The intention was evidently to build a whole series of paired 3-storey houses in the terrace style, punctuated by single-storey entrances, somewhat in the manner of the Paragon at Blackheath.

A lease of 1805 mentions land fronting south on Canonbury Lane and partly east, "on an intended square designed to be called Canonbury Square". Yet by 1809 only four leases (not necessarily for single houses) had been granted to Leroux and one other lessee, and funds were running out. It has been suggested that the then likely further development of Highbury Fields might have provided unwelcome competition; at all events by 1809 Leroux was bankrupt. In the *London Gazette* of 1810 he is named as "Henry Jacob Leroux, of Canonbury Square, builder", and that June part of his property was auctioned in Sebbon's Buildings at the Angel.

By that time the land had been bisected for the laying out of a new and important carriage-way, linking the turnpike road from the corner of Highbury Place with the parish of St Leonard's Shoreditch, through land leased to the farmers Samuel Rhodes and Richard Laycock by the Clothworkers' Company, the Earl of Northampton, and the New River Company. This highway, called New North Road, from the outset interfered with the quiet of the rudimentary 'square', carving through the very centre of Leroux's building plot — an early example of traffic concerns overriding other local interests. It opened in 1812, but supposing the road to have been some time in plan, it might have affected the economics of Leroux's venture. It certainly spoiled the unity of the new square's north side, then partly built.

*He became 1st Marquess in 1812.

Canonbury Square, NE side in 1945 (nos. 33-39)
Nos. 36-38 (far left) were damaged in World War II and rebuilt in 1954

All this suggests no great pressure to build or buy in the area, and indeed only after the end of the Napoleonic Wars did the real demand begin. Even by 1818, when the second part of Leroux's site was disposed of (behind Compton Terrace, up to the edge of Canonbury Tavern grounds), probably only a few houses existed 'in carcass'.

In 1819 building resumed in Compton Terrace (q.v.). Development of Canonbury Square was now largely determined by Laycock, as chief land-owner in the area and Leroux's assignee. In 1821 Laycock agreed with Lord Northampton to build on the south and east sides of the square, and south of Canonbury Place, up to New North Road and Lower Road and including some adjoining roads. In November he had supposedly begun the terraces on the south side of the square, and was to equip them with sewers within the next year. His houses in the New North Road (now Canonbury Road), known as Albion Terrace and Northampton Place until 1835, were of similar size, and he also built some more modest terraces, Canonbury Grove and Canonbury Terrace (now Alwyne Villas). None of this appears in the Rate Books before 1826, and even then they were largely marked 'Empty'. The east side of the square is recorded with two houses in 1827, four in 1829 and the rest in 1830. A further rash of building took place in the 1840s, and by the 1850s the estate was substantially built over (see *Alwyne Square*), the period of development covering about 90 years from the first appearance of John Dawes.

Canonbury Square and district were now at the height of prosperity; but like other parts of Islington, from the 1860s the area began to decline, largely because of the exodus along the railways to newer, more rural suburbs. Inhabitants of the professional class gave way to lower social strata: legal and commercial clerks, craftsmen jewellers and watchmakers, and even the humbler bricklayers and plasterers. Although pockets of prosperity survived, the district reached a nadir of poverty between the two World Wars.

During the war parts of Canonbury were destroyed by bombs, including the north-east section of Canonbury Square. By the 1950s, living in the square was in the nature of slumming, the good old houses run down and the streets gas-lit and seedy. Soon after the war the 6th Marquess of Northampton decided to sell much of his estate, and since 1951 the residual estate has been administered by P. Broomhall and Partners, while trusts were formed chiefly for the Marquess's son and heir.

The purchasers, Western Ground Rents, developed part of their property, and the gaps caused by bombing were rebuilt, chiefly by Louis de Soissons, but John Spencer Square and the north side of Canonbury Square were by their architect-surveyor Nash. Erection of the new houses from 1954 generally renewed interest from the professional middle classes, but by a stroke of irony they were invited to view the new development, and stayed to occupy the old. From then dates the gradual renaissance of Canonbury and later, by osmosis, of Barnsbury and the other parts of south Islington.

In the 1970s the Northampton family re-acquired part of the property, including much of the south side of the square, retaining the freehold while selling leaseholds of flats. In this way the ownership situation reverted to some extent to the way it was before the war.

Architecture

Canonbury Square is really a rectangle, and for most of its existence has been split by the New North Road. Because of this cleavage, it can be considered in six, or even seven parts. The different building dates resulted in distinct differences in style, and all the terraces are detached from each other.

Earliest and grandest is Henry Leroux's NW range, a fine '2nd-class' terrace in dark brick with extremely long drawing-room windows, consisting of nos. 42–45, and nos. 46–47 with different fenestration. No. 47 now exists only to ground-floor level and has become part of no. 46. Even the existing floor is a pastiche post-war rebuild: the original building, occupied since 1921 on a 3-yearly and then yearly tenancy by the Comrades of the Great War (later renamed the Canonbury Ex-Servicemen's Club), was demolished in 1937. A local story, plausible if unsubstantiated, is that the Marquess, who had wanted to get rid of these tenants for some time, in the end could only do so by declaring the building unsafe and pulling it down.

The original builders of this side of the square were of varying quality, and inferior bricklayers on the party walls failed to bond them into the better-built façades. Eventually, therefore, the front walls bowed out and, in the 1950s, had to be reconstructed. The style of the houses nearer the New North Road corner is similar to those on the New River estate, the windows lower with sunk brick surrounds and a string-course, and stuccoed ground floors (nos. 40, 40a, 41).

The rest of the north side, and the two single houses, Northampton Lodge (no. 39) adjoining Canonbury Road, and no. 48 on the west side, are mysteriously undocumented, though all seem to pre-date 1818: identification is obscured by the Rate Books' lumping of the whole area prior to 1826, and many houses even until 1829, indiscriminately as "Canonbury" or "Canonbury Lane". No. 48, a double-fronted villa with French-looking first-floor windows and a large stucco-surrounded front door with rusticated keystones, is a taller, dignified version of the Cloudesley Square brick boxes. It has a large garden at the side and also, alone of the square's houses except for Northampton Lodge, a minute front garden, all other houses having sunk areas. In 1987 the house was gutted and heavily restored.

The impressive Northampton Lodge is a handsome gentleman's villa with extensive back garden, and the added grandeur of low convex wings containing single-storey rooms or conservatories. Exhaustive search backwards through the Rate Books establishes that the house existed in 1811, empty, and from 1812–23 was occupied by Mr William Eley, from 1824–5 by Mr John Scott, from 1826–40 by Mrs Elizabeth Whalley, and then by Major Robert Holborn. Before 1811 identification is

Northampton Lodge, Canonbury Square in 1968

doubtful, as the valuation appears to have changed, but the house may have been built by 1807, in which case it might be assigned to Henry Leroux; the fact that it then lay empty for some years does not suggest its having been commissioned.

The five houses constituting nos. 37–39 are post-war infilling by Nash for Western Ground Rents in a rather spindly terrace style, with end 'pavilions'. The irregular group beyond, nos. 33–36, also traceable to at least 1818, were presumably the work of individual builders, their windows asymmetrical (no. 33A is pastiche by Christopher Libby 1980s).

The SW terrace (nos. 1–12), built above cellars on a raised pavement, Bath or Clifton style, to maintain the building level where the ground falls away, is in the Rate Books from 1823, though not completed until 1829 (nos. 10–12). Like the square's other terraces its first-floor windows, above a broad cill band, are in sunk arched recesses, New River style. But its ground floor is distinctive, with segmental windows in matching arches, and the two pairs of end houses and two central houses (nos. 1 and 2, 11 and 12, 6 and 7), stuccoed with window keystones were all evidently intended for timber columned porticoes, though only the central pair exist. The windows have Gothicky panes. Fanlights are teardrop style, area railings orthodox urn and halberd, but contrasting railings of lattice design flank the front steps.

The SE range (13–24) and east side (25–32) first appear in Rate Books in 1826 and 1827 respectively, both named Marquis Terrace, oddly since they are at right angles and do not even meet at the corner. The east side started very slowly and nos. 25–28 seem to have been completed only in 1830. These are two orthodox terraces, ground floors mostly stuccoed and New-River-style first floors. Nos. 17–20 have a full top storey above a coping, the rest of the row having only attics. Nos. 25–32 are a flat, boxy block, tall and longitudinal, lacking features or cornices, but the ground-floor windows are set in circular-headed recesses with keystones where stuccoed. In converting these houses to flats some years ago some of the front doors were unfortunately taken out of use and closed. No 25's doorway is rather botched by its original builders, pressed against the stuccoing of the next house. No. 32 is entered from the side. No. 28 bears a name-plaque, blank. Most of both these terraces (nos. 12–18 and all the E side) have pretty oval motifs to the balconies.

Gardens

The 4th Marquess was the first land-owner to open his private square-gardens to the public, in Clerkenwell and Canonbury. Canonbury was formally opened in 1884 by Lord Brabazon, Chairman of the Public Gardens, Boulevards and Playgrounds Association. In the east garden the small statue of a young girl, originally from Italy, was presented to the Council in 1943 by Mr Stokes, of 343 Essex Road. The railings, of course, were uprooted during the war and replaced by chicken-wire netting, but already in 1946 the Council included the square gardens in a plan to rehabilitate more than 20 open spaces in Islington. The railings took longer to replace. Early in the 1950s the gardens were laid out, and in 1956 the Londoner's Diary in the *Evening Standard* claimed Canonbury as "London's most beautiful square" (24 May). It can certainly claim to be Islington's most beautiful, retaining its charm and atmosphere, though the heavily trafficked New North Road has for many years had an effect on the surroundings which its builders in 1812 could never have anticipated.

Inhabitants
At no. 8 from 1844–66 lived Samuel Phelps, the famous actor-manager of Sadler's Wells (he then removed to 420 Camden Road until his death in 1878). Under him Sadler's Wells reached its pinnacle of Victorian fame when in those unlikely surroundings he staged all of Shakespeare's plays to packed audiences.

At no. 18 from 1837 lived George Daniel, bibliophile and antiquarian book collector (1789–1864).

No. 39, Northampton Lodge, from 1840–52 was occupied by Major Robert Holborn, an Islington-born tea merchant, who married Sarah, daughter of Daniel Curling, then the resident of Canonbury House. Another bibliophile, he later employed as librarian for his large collection Henry W. Fincham, who became Librarian of the Order of St John at St John's Gate. Major Holborn died in 1892 at 11 Highbury Crescent (q.v.).

At no. 36, the home from 1844 of the Rev. Arthur Johnson, who kept a school there for many years, Joseph Chamberlain, MP (1836–1914) was a pupil.

In a second-floor flat at no. 17A, Evelyn Waugh lived as a young man, from 1928– 30. At no. 27B George Orwell lived from 1945 until his death in 1950, with his wife and adopted child. Next door, no. 26A during the 1950s was the home of Duncan Grant and Vanessa Bell.

Cloudesley Square (1826)

"The greatest spur to building in the neighbourhood", writes Samuel Lewis in 1842, was "the letting of the Stonefield estate on building leases in the year 1824: which led to the formation of Cloudesley-square, Cloudesley-terrace and the adjoining streets". Early in the century the Barnsbury area had almost no houses, and during less than 20 years before Lewis was writing (he says), "two-thirds of the surface of the district [were] covered with streets and buildings". Cloudesley square was the earliest of the Barnsbury squares to be built.

The Cloudesley estate was part of Barnsbury manor, and was also known as the Stonefield or Stoneyfield, or 14 Acres estate (actually 16 acres, 3 roods and 22 perches). The long, narrow site lay between the Back Road and the meandering hill-top lane through White Conduit Fields – now Thornhill Road – that bordered

Cloudesley Square and Holy Trinity Church
From a postcard view of *c*. 1910

the Thornhill estate on the west. In the early 16th century it had been owned by Sir Richard Cloudesley who, dying in 1517, left an enigmatic will making generous donations to the parish but decreeing, rather significantly, that the priest pray thrice weekly "for my sowle and all Christen sowles" and that a *De profundis* be said for his soul with every mass. His body was popularly believed to lie disturbed in his grave, as related in "The Islington Ghost", a penny pamphlet (1842): his tomb was indeed kept up by the parish, and several times repaired or newly built.

Sir Richard may or may not have hoped to buy salvation, but he certainly benefited posterity through his land's increasing profits, whose income was duly distributed to the poor by the Mayor and Vicar of Islington, and later also by the chairman of the Royal Northern Hospital and by trustees for the parish's Anglican churches and for hospitals and charities serving the sick poor. Whereas in 1760 the distributed profits were £60, two centuries later they had risen to nearly £10,000.

Early in the 19th century the parish's tenant of the estate was the rich local dairy farmer, Samuel Rhodes (great-grandfather of Cecil Rhodes). In 1809 the Corporation of London cast eyes on the land during one of the several abortive attempts to remove Smithfield cattle market from near the city to a more salubrious site; but the proposal fell through. The estate was then valued at nearly £23,000. (Lewis 126) By then, however, Islington's dairying days were numbered, and the rich pickings of bricks and mortar could be foreseen. In 1811 an Act was passed enabling the trustees to grant building leases, and by the next year the terrace now numbered 71– 79 Liverpool Road (not part of the Cloudesley estate) had been built (Hol. & Fins. Sewer Rate Books). At that time a private bill was before Parliament for building a Chapel of Ease for the already growing parish of St Mary's. In January 1811 the Stonefield trustees had put it to the Vestry that by letting their estate on building leases, "considerable income would be derived", which could be devoted "materially to ease" the burden on ratepayers in raising the funds required to build the Chapel of Ease; and they secured approval for their applying to Parliament for such permission.

The trustees got as far as laying the drainage, at a cost of £1,159.18.11, and making a plan for building on the estate, and the Chapel of Ease (St Mary Magdalene, designed by William Wickings) was built that year – at considerably greater cost than estimated, which caused uproar in the Vestry. But no further progress was made at that time on the Stonefield estate, and there were no takers for building leases until 1818. The parish, however, then began building on the adjacent Glebe Land, and Elizabeth Terrace (now Cloudesley Place) was built in 1821, marked by a date-stone.

About 1818 building started along the Liverpool Road frontage of the estate, a Pentonville carpenter, John Emmett, having taken most of these leases. He acquired the rest of the site in three separate leases dated 1824–6, by 1825 his Cloudesley Square, as the focal point, had been laid out, and the Stonefield or Cloudesley estate was completed in 1825 and 1826. Lewis names five builders in all for the estate, of whom one, Philip Langhorn, appears however to have done very little. Of the rest, Richard Chapman had developed the Glebe land; two streets were named after him (now Ritchie and Batchelor Streets), but in 1830 he went bankrupt. David Sage, and to a lessor extent Dorset Goepel, built Upper and Lower Islington Terraces, now Cloudesley Road.

The straggling site offered little scope except for these long terraces flanking a central square, parallel with the Barnsbury Road and Liverpool Road terraces, with another long street, Stonefield Street, bisecting the square. When the church was built this street was treated separately as Stonefield and Cloudesley Streets, while two lateral arms linked the square with Liverpool and Cloudesley Roads.

The small square, thus entered at the centre of each side, was eccentric in forming an irregular hexagon, allowing for slightly wider houses at the flattened western angles. Two boxy free-standing villas, not remarkably elegant, flank the east entrant. For these, stables were planned if not actually built, in the spaces alongside to north and south. The northern house was later connected to the adjoining terrace at ground level, the other still has a long wide garden, leaving the square oddly open at that point.

Square and estate are now largely cut off from through traffic by barriers at most exits, but the streets, otherwise still mostly unspoilt, suffer not from traffic but from parked cars.

In 1937 the bulk of the estate was auctioned, the trust retaining its interest only in the SW quadrant, bounded by the present Cloudesley Place and Road, and the west sides of the square and of Cloudesley Street. The rents were not enough to cover maintenance or improvement costs, and in the 1970s the trustees sold several long leaseholds with repairing covenants, since when upkeep on the estate as a whole has greatly improved and the remaining houses have been upgraded with changes in tenancies.

Early in this century Dove Brothers, builders of 19 new churches in Islington though not, it so happens, of Holy Trinity in the square, rebuilt certain properties as their offices in Cloudesley Place. Their removal from this long-established base, and impending termination of the lease of their stonemason subsidiaries, Gilbert & Turnbull, may affect future development of the estate.

Architecture:
The terraced houses, of 3 floors and basements, are in the attractive New River estate style, ground floor fronts of grooved stucco with round-headed features, and first-floor windows in round-headed recesses linked by string courses. The detached villas' boxy effect, however, is echoed in the unbroken brick fronts above the top-floor windows, concealing the usual valley gutters. All houses have balconies, mostly double, of a pretty interlaced segment design; the railings are standard, with halberd finials.

Holy Trinity Church (1826–9)
This was a Commissioners' church, intended further to relieve St Mary's in what was seen to be a growing district. Mr Savage, probably John Savage (1779–1852) – a Hackney-born architect who started by designing bridges and later worked on numerous churches in London and elsewhere – notably St Luke's, Chelsea (1820–24) – was the Commissioners' first choice of architect, and his plans, under consideration for some months (1825), were even approved, but the tenders did not agree with his estimates, and it was the young Charles Barry (1795–1860) whose plans were finally adopted, in March 1826. Barry similarly secured the assignment for Islington's other two new churches of this date, St Paul's, Ball's Pond and St John's, Upper Holloway, both of which have towers and externally are replicas of one another.

At Holy Trinity, Barry worked in the newly fashionable Perpendicular style, producing a recognisable if cheap brick copy of King's College Chapel, Cambridge. He was highly praised for his three Islington churches, the parish's first Gothic exercise: William Wickings's St Mary Magdalene, the chapel-of-ease in the Holloway Road, designed in 1812, had been in the then customary 'brick box' style, with plain classical round-headed windows; and in neighbouring Clerkenwell, Chadwell Mylne's St Mark's (1826–8), though graced with a Gothic tower, was still

Holy Trinity Church and part of the north side of Cloudesley Square
The church by the young Charles Barry (1826-9) echoes the style of King's
College Chapel, Cambridge
From a contemporary engraving

48

a rectangular box. Only from the late 1830s did a rash of Gothic churches start to cover the parish, well in the wake of Barry's triple experiments. Holy Trinity was commended by the vicar, the Rev. Daniel Wilson, in his opening sermon there (1829) as a "noble, magnificent, yet simple" building which "proves demonstrably that . . . the Pointed may be executed, with a sufficient portion of ornament for a parochial Church or Chapel, at a comparatively small cost".

The tower-less Holy Trinity internally resembled Barry's other two churches in style and plan, of nave with shortened sides; but its chancel was wider. The most distinctive feature is the large West window balanced by two octagonal towerlets, King's chapel fashion — sadly lacking on the E front with only small cupolas and caps — that being the end visible from the "high road" (Liverpool Road), for which the *Gentleman's Magazine* critic gravely reproved the architect (May 1829).

More unfortunate, perhaps, is the failure to provide an eye-catching feature, such as a more elaborate porch, to punctuate the north side seen from Stonefield Street — possibly for lack of funds, although the church cost £11,535, a generous sum compared with many that followed later.

Holy Trinity remained adequate to serve the new district only until the 1850s, when Islington's spectacularly rising population outstripped its capacity, and in 1852 the parish authorised a further new church, St Andrew's, to serve the rapidly growing west Barnsbury in the new Thornhill estate.

A century later the churches' fortunes were reversed, and during the 1960s Holy Trinity was among those declared redundant. After remaining empty for some time, with occasional use for concerts (for which its acoustics were not particularly successful), in 1980 it was leased and refurbished by a Pentecostal sect with a largely African congregation, as the Celestial Church of Christ. The railings have been restored.

In 1867 the chancel had been remodelled; in 1903 the church was restored, at a cost of £3000, and the north and south galleries removed. The handsome E window by Thomas Willement commemorates Sir Richard Cloudesley, with his portrait, kneeling, in the centre, below a canopy, with a long inscription on his donation.

Inhabitants: Cloudesley Square's history has been unspectacular. At no. 10 lived Thomas Edwards (b. 1779), compiler of the English/Welsh Dictionary in 1850, and here he died in 1858. At no. 33 in 1864 lived the writer and social reformer George Linnaeus Banks (1821–81) and his wife Isabella, poet and novelist (1821–97).

Colebrooke Row and Duncan Terrace (*c.* 1717–1842)

Note:
The building history of these terraces is exceptionally complex and, especially at the north end, there is discrepancy between surviving leases and the rate books. Frank

Kelsall, to whose first investigation of the area for the GLC Historic Buildings Division in 1967 I am greatly indebted, remarks on the discrepancy in the records, and until more leases can be examined in detail – perhaps not even then – there remain gaps in our knowledge. Subsequent alterations, apparently undocumented (such as to nos. 58 and 59 Colebrooke Row, and to Lamb's Cottage) complicate the issue further. The long-drawn-out building process, covering more than a century, in itself is not easy to follow; and confusion is not lessened by the re-naming of individual terraces – especially as 1–3 Colebrooke Row started life as Duncan Place, and 50–58 Duncan Terrace ("New Terrace") as Colebrooke Terrace.

Colebrooke Row is an example of piecemeal, unplanned development, at first taking advantage of an amenity – here the man-made New River – and ending as a harmonious group of buildings enjoying a park-like, if not square-like environment. Starting haphazardly with isolated houses and even industrial connections at the north end, it first develops with an unadorned continuous row (32–53), and only later in varying forms of designed terrace: James Taylor's sparely elegant New Terrace, followed soon after with other examples of standard 'terrace' style with central and end houses advanced or otherwise distinguished, some in the style familiar in the New River estate, with upper windows framed in recessed arches; and later with William Watkins's elaborations of 'pavilion' ends in rusticated stucco.

Building history

The order in which the surviving houses were built was as follows:

	Colebrooke Row	Duncan Terrace
Pre-1730	56–59 Colebrooke Row	
c. 1745, 1755	54, 55 Colebrooke Row	
1767–74	60–65 Colebrooke Row (Bird's Buildings)	
1768, 1772–4	34–36 and 41–53 Colebrooke Row (37–40 demolished)	
1760s?		64 Duncan Terrace (Colebrooke Cottage)
1791–2		50–58 Duncan Terrace (= New Terrace, later Colebrooke Terrace) and Charlton Place/Charlton Crescent
1793		46–49 Duncan Terrace

	Colebrooke Row	Duncan Terrace
1798–1803		2–10 Duncan Terrace (1 demolished)
c. 1798–9 & 1803	389 City Road and 1–3 Colebrooke Row (River Terrace)	
1814	4–5 Colebrooke Row (6–10 demolished)	
c. 1820		11–14 Duncan Terrace (and ?59 & 60 Duncan Terrace, demolished)
?1829, 1833/4		16–32 Duncan Terrace
1834	Islington Presbyterian Church (demolished)	Irvingite Church, Duncan St (demolished)
1836		Islington Proprietary School (demolished; site of County Court)
1837	13–19 Colebrooke Row (River Terrace N.)	
1838	11 & 12 Colebrooke Row (demolished)	
1841	20–28 Colebrooke Row (Montagu Place)	St John the Evangelist Church
c. 1841		34–45 Duncan Terrace
c. 1880		61–63 Duncan Terrace

Architecture

The buildings are discussed in descending number order, starting from the north end. Nos. 60–65 (Bird's Buildings) are not included.

1) Brick kilns and nurseries

The village of Islington clustered round its High Street and Green, and continued northwards along the two branching high roads, Upper Street past the parish church and, more stragglingly, the Lower Street or Essex Road. The village, lying uphill from the City, was ringed with fine pasture land, good for the dairy herds bred by increasingly rich farmer–landowners of the Rhodes and Pocock families.

Just behind the High Street, a southern extension of Highbury Manor stretched a long finger of grassland towards the Angel, with a small detached piece near the Angel itself, separated from the rest by land of the Prebendal Manor of Islington. This last estate originally belonging to the Prebends or Canons of St Paul's, but with no manor house: much of it eventually became the Clothworkers' and Packington estates (see Arlington Square). The local soil proved good for builder's clay, and the Prebendal lands were dug for brick-making as early as the 14th century; in the 16th the kilns and brickworks were said to have been a great resort of rogues and vagabonds. [Nelson, 1829, p.112]

From early in the 17th century the New River took its course through the westerly part of these two manorial lands, and it was along the river banks that to-day's almost continuous Duncan Terrace and Colebrooke Row came to be built over a period of more than a century. For many decades a large gap separated the terraces at the north and south ends.

In late mediaeval times the Hattersfield, part of a close on this land, had been bought by King Edward IV's household treasurer, Sir John Elrington, one of whose descendants sold it, and in 1613 – the year of the New River's completion – it passed to the Miller family. A Miller descendant sold it in 1717 to Walter Burton, a glazier, who built a brewhouse, brick kilns and associated houses on the land; but in 1727 re-sold it to James Colebrooke, Lord of the Manor of Highbury and Islington's greatest land-owner. Colebrooke leased part of the field to a carpenter, Samuel Steemson. The documentation is contradictory, but the first houses seem to have been built by Burton in or after 1717, and later by Steemson, not far from the northern tip of Islington Green, where the New River emerged from a tunnel running diagonally under the Lower Road. One of the earliest (now no. 57) was a public house with tea gardens, presumably at the rear, run for some years as "The Castle", and mentioned in no. 26 of *The Connoisseur* in 1757 [Lewis 352].

Some two acres of the property named Buttfield lay on the east side of the river. Sir George Colebrooke, James's youngest son, who inherited the estate in 1761, bridged the river, made a road across the field (apparently *not* River Lane, now St Peter's Street, which existed by 1717), and leased out a strip of land on the east bank, on which a row of houses was built in 1768 and 1772/4. This was the original Colebrooke Row. But in 1773 Sir George became bankrupt, and the property was again sold.

By 1770, however, a new use for the good local soil had been found. Two brothers, William and John Watson, leased six acres of Hattersfield from Sir George, on part of which they planted a nursery garden specialising in exotics, and built a hot-house and greenhouse. In 1771 they exchanged plants with the Chelsea Physic Garden. James Watson withdrew from the partnership in 1785, and William died in 1792; a third brother, Thomas, became the first grower in Britain to succeed in coaxing a flower from a new importation from the Crimea, the Pontic azalea (1798). [VCH 72; nursery ad.] He also increased the size of the garden, which eventually covered $5\frac{1}{2}$ acres.

Meanwhile Islington's dairy farms had also increased in size, and by the early 19th century the Rhodes family owned some 400 acres of hay-fields and dairy cattle. In about 1800 Samuel Rhodes took over a farm on the site of the present Duncan Street

Colebrooke Row, north end, in the 18th century
showing the Revd Mr Rule's school, and "Starvation Farm" by the New River
From a 19th-century water-colour by C. H. Matthews

from its long-time owners, the Pullin family, and it became one of the London area's largest dairy farms, with a high reputation for quality. The rich fodder it produced was evidenced by the large haystacks made up every summer round the south end of Colebrooke Terrace — though in 1835, when Cromwell wrote, nurseries and meadows alike had for some dozen years been "broken up" for brick-making.

Ever since Walter Burton built his kilns in the 1720s, Hattersfield had commonly been known as "Tile-Kiln Field", and by 1769 round Bird's Buildings, the northern extension of Colebrooke Row, another kiln had been established by Thomas Bird. Samuel Rhodes was not long in taking advantage of the clay's potential. The nursery, now owned by John Eddington, was too valuable a site to escape, and closed in 1824; in 1827 the ground was sold to Thomas Cubitt, who built houses on part of River Lane, and in and after 1843 sold the rest to the then farmer, James Rhodes. Another name foreshadowing the great building push that followed the Napoleonic Wars was that of Mr Gerard Noel, who already owned a large field south of the New River and in 1810 bought three acres of Hattersfield between the New River and the High Street. It was after him that Noel and Gerrard Roads are named.

For some 30 years the nursery gardens were dug up to become brickfields, and when the clay was exhausted and the land at a premium, houses were built.

2) *Starvation Farm*

In the late 18th century one farm achieved an unhappy notoriety. It occupied the west bank of the New River, near where it emerged from the Lower Street tunnel, and its site curiously remained almost open until the 1980s. It was owned by Baron Ephraim Lopez Pereira D'Aguilar, a rich Portuguese Jew born in 1740 in Vienna, whose father had settled in England.

D'Aguilar became a naturalised Englishman, made two rich marriages in succession, and for a time lived in great style in the City. Then, however, he lost much American property because of the War of Independence, and his second marriage proved a failure. The Baron, still quite young, withdrew from respectable society and became to put it charitably, eccentric – or less charitably, mean. "Rude, slovenly, and careless", says Nelson, "both in his person and manners." Among other cruelties, he was said to have kept his wife locked up in a hay-loft, and although he lost a legal action on this, had the effrontery to appeal that she share the costs.

D'Aguilar's main dwelling was in Shaftesbury Place off Aldersgate Street, but he spent the day-time at a house in Islington, at 21 Camden Street, to which "a sort of farm" was attached. Strange tales were told of his ménage, to which he was said to lure orphans and destitute women under guise of protection or employment, in fact keeping a kind of harem of concubines with their assorted offspring, which exhibited (Nelson again) "a scene of the most abandoned depravity". He also owned property in other villages – Bethnal Green, Twickenham, Sydenham – filled with furniture but kept locked up and inhabited only by starving caretakers. Keeping farms was one of his idiosyncrasies, but that did not extend to caring for animals, and the farm beside the New River was "a perfect dunghill". Heaped with filth, its untended yard was littered with the dying and dead carcases of starving animals, to whom he doled out the minimum of fodder until the wretched beasts were reduced to cannibalism. Indignant locals would pelt the baron as he shuffled about in filthy, shoddy clothes, and the New River Company threatened a prosecution for allowing the decaying corpse of one of his cattle to pollute the stream.

Though said to be generous to the poor – from dubious motives – D'Aguilar was at odds with his two daughters and their husbands, accusing them of being "too fine", and in his last illness he turned away one daughter with oaths, refusing a doctor or even a fire. This was at his Aldersgate Street house, where he died in 1802, aged 62, and was buried at Mile End. A two-day auction of his Islington estate realised only £128 for the emaciated cattle and £7 for a rotting coach kept on the premises; but his jewels, plate and stock of merchandise such as cochineal and indigo fetched large sums, and the total value of his various properties proved more than £200,000. [Nelson 386–92; Cromwell 179–84; Lewis 354-5] The yard alongside the New River bank was for many years afterwards still known locally as "The Farm". It is now a small mews development, created by Christopher Libby in 1981.

3) Early houses and occupants

By the time of Baron D'Aguilar's death Colebrooke Row had long taken shape opposite his farm. Nos. 58 and 59, at right angles to the "Castle" tavern but then standing clear, may have been part of the contemporary property sold to James Colebrooke in 1727. Their interiors, less altered than the exteriors, suggest their having been built together. The two were knocked into one, probably in the 1750s when they were converted into a school for young gentlemen, run for some 40 years by the Revd John Rule and later by Mr Philip Nuttingley. As an academy – Islington was thick with them – it seems to have been chiefly noted for its dramatic performances when the boys broke up for holidays. One of these even got (privately) into print in 1768, a translation from Marivaux under the name *The Agreeable Surprize*, published in a volume with the even more agreeable title *Poetical Blossoms, or the Sports of Genius; being a Collection of Poems upon several Subjects, by the young Gentlemen of Mr Rule's Academy at Islington*, price 1s. 6d. [Nelson 385]

At the house adjoining the Castle (no. 56), Colly Cibber the dramatist and pillar of Sadler's Wells Theatre lodged towards the end of his life, dying in 1757. For 27 years, despite or perhaps because of his uninspired verse, he had been Poet Laureate to King George II. The career of his daughter Charlotte is a sad chronicle of failure. After a pampered but tomboyish upbringing, to her father's undying displeasure she married a ne'er-do-well violinist called Richard Charke, and after this predictably proved a disaster, she snatched a precarious living as strolling actress, hack journalist, grocer, and quack doctor marketing improbable cures. At one time she worked the puppets for Mr Russell at the "Great Room" in Brewer Street (now Paget Street), Clerkenwell. An anonymous "literary man" who visited her in destitution described her as struggling to write her autobiography with a stump of a pen and a broken teacup as inkwell, in "a wretched thatched hovel in Clerkenwell", and in these distressed circumstances the poor soul died only three years after her unrelenting father (1760). (Cromwell, p. 178)

Poor Charlotte Charke: had she lived a century or so later, she might have benefited from the hostel run for working women at 28 Duncan Terrace – or one even closer to her father's, advertised at an unspecified date at 55 Colebrooke Row.

In 1768 the handsome terrace of Colebrooke Row was begun from which the whole street eventually took its name. The site was leased by Sir George Colebrooke to Josiah Collins, bricklayer of Seven Dials. In September/October Collins built the north end (now nos. 53–50), presumably 'in carcase', and then took a lease on a further 400 feet southwards as far as the present Gerrard Road, and soon built "several new houses" on to no. 50 (as recorded in the 1768 Rate Book). Two more followed at the south end, leaving a space (nos. 33, 32), the first, larger and grander, probably intended by Collins for himself; the second carried the date-stone, 1768, for the row. Both were demolished in 1952.

Nos. 34-55 Colebrooke Row in 1966
The original row was nos. 34-53 (1768-74). The Victorianised no. 54
(foreground) has since been restored

Collins built nine houses in all, nos. 53–47 and the detached 33, 32, but they were slow to let: in 1771 only no. 50 was occupied, and although nos. 53–47 were tenanted by 1772, all were mortgaged and re-mortgaged, and Collins went bankrupt. Sir George, too, was now in financial difficulties, obliged to mortgage his Islington property for £100,000 and later to sell the freeholds. That year Richard Masefield, paper stainer of the Strand, leased the rest of the ground from him (purchasing the freehold in 1775), on which he caused to be built the rest of the row, nos. 34–46, leaving a narrow gap between his end house, no. 34, and Collins's no. 33. The builder of six of these is named as John Hetley, but neither he nor any other is named as lessee.

Masefield leased out nos. 35–37 in September 1774 (only no. 35 survives); by November 1776 the other nine (38–46) were also let, but at once mortgaged back to Masefield, who seems to have been a prosperous speculator. The houses still remained empty.

No. 32, the end house (no. 1 in its original numbering) was first leased to John Yeomans, a carpenter; it was run as a public house, the Colebrooke Arms; later became a girls' boarding school; by 1828 it was another young gentlemen's academy, and in the 1860s was again a young ladies' school.

Secluded within a walled garden behind the south end of Colebrooke Row was a small white-plastered house which, though built by the mid-18th century, does not appear in any version of Dent's map, and whose origin is unknown. Here from 1772 to 1776 lived William Woodfall (1746–1803), a man of many talents who became a celebrated Parliamentary reporter. He was at first apprenticed to a bookseller, worked on his father's paper the *Public Advertiser*, ran away to become an actor, married, returned to London in 1772 and settled for a few years in Colebrooke Row. He turned to journalism and edited a couple of papers, and, developing a remarkably retentive memory, took to reporting House of Commons debates. On one famous occasion (1789) he was said to have sat absorbing the speeches for several hours, without making notes, and have then written them up – in 16 columns – in time for the MPs at breakfast next morning. However, his *Diary* or Parliamentary Report was superseded by Hansard, and instead Woodfall became a respected drama critic; though all this was long after his brief sojourn in Islington.

His modest house, on the stretch then known only as "Lower Side", and later numbered 32A Colebrooke Row, remained little altered. From 1831–7 it was occupied as a Police Station, and more than a century later an old inhabitant of the area recalled its still having been known as "the Old Court House". Not long after the Second World War it became ruinous, and was unfortunately demolished with the adjoining nos. 32 and 33 in 1952.

4) *New building of the 1790s*
So far, apart from Colebrooke Cottage, an isolated house near D'Aguilar's farm (see (6) below), building had been confined to east of the New River, but in 1790 and

Woodfall's Cottage, Colebrooke Row
From a water-colour of 1840

1791 there was a flurry of building opposite Colebrooke Row of a modern, elegant kind. Sir George Colebrooke's sale of land in the 1770s to ease his ailing fortunes had included part of Clay Pit Field, bought by a Robert Vincent. In 1790 Vincent partly re-sold to James Taylor, a young surveyor and builder (*c.* 1765–1846) whose office was in York Place, a terrace in the City Road.

Taylor shortly built nine houses on a raised pavement which he called "New Terrace" – new *vis-à-vis* Colebrooke Row, that is – (date-stone 1791), leasing them to two carpenters, a glazier, a mason and a timber merchant; he also built the north side of Charlton Place (date-stone 1790). New Terrace (now 50–58 Duncan Terrace) was also confusingly, though not illogically, known as Colebrooke Terrace after the original owner of the site. In 1793 Taylor bought more of Clay Pit Field to the south and continued the line of New Terrace (nos. 46–49 Duncan Terrace) on the other side of his new Charlton Place. He also built Charlton Crescent to face Charlton Place, the shape perhaps chosen in order to squeeze another house or two from the site. The leases are dated 1794.

Taylor, who was a Roman Catholic, was at this time living at Greenwich, where also in 1791 he built Park Place and, the following year, a Catholic chapel in East Street, a result of the Catholic Relief Act of 1791 which raised the embargo on such building: following this, Taylor built several others and also institutions, such as the original buildings for St Cuthbert's College at Ushaw, Co. Durham (1804–8).

Other builders to whom Sir George Colebrooke sold his freeholds included William and later Edward Cross; Cross Street, much of which was built in the 1760s/70s, and whose façades and doorcases resemble those in Colebrooke Row, is a result of their investment.

Soon after James Taylor's west-bank activities, building began alongside the New River adjoining the City Road. On the west side in 1798/9 a few houses appeared on land belonging to a gentleman named Gold, a plot which seems to have been out-with the extensive Rhodes family property in the area. Without considerable further research into leases it is extremely difficult to make sense of the evidence here between maps and Rate Books. As the *Gentleman's Magazine* of January 1799 reveals (see p. 60), building began in 1798, and Dent's 1805/6 map shows "Duncan Terrace", a row of 10 houses on Gold's land. The houses appear also on Horwood's map of 1799; all were occupied by 1803.

On the east side Dent, but not Horwood, also shows three houses, where the land belonged to Mr John Graham. The Rate Books, however, in which already four houses appear by 1799, eight by 1800, lump all these and the ones on Gold's land together as "Duncan Place". By 1804/5 the number has risen to 14, some unfinished, and from 1808 "Duncan Place" has become "Duncan Terrace" (i.e. west side), while the last three houses listed and two new ones are re-identified as "River Terrace" (i.e. east side); they included the present 389 City Road. In 1814 River Terrace has acquired more houses: these were among houses demolished in 1960.

5) The Regent's Canal – and a Non-Railway
Between these new terraces and Colebrooke Row, nursery gardens were still flourishing when from 1813 to 1816 John Nash's Regent's Canal was being tunnelled through Pentonville Hill. This product of the new industrial age was dug under the New River, to emerge on its east side and thence pass through a last lock before widening into the City Road basin. Construction of the 970-yard tunnel below the river as well as under surrounding roads and houses was a considerable engineering feat, and as recently as 1812 Rennie's attempt to burrow a road through Highgate HIll had ended in disaster when the structure collapsed. Nash's Highgate Archway was the answer to that; a solution not available to him in building the canal. His Islington tunnel, $17\frac{1}{2}$ feet across, was just wide enough to admit the passage of a barge but not a towpath, so that at the Muriel Street entrance in Barnsbury the barge-horses had to be unhitched and led along the streets to rejoin the boat at the eastern end, while the bargees, lying on their backs, 'legged' the boat through the tunnel by thrusting their feet against the brick walls.

After 1826 a steam-tug was used to tow a string of barges in convoy, working by a chain laid along the canal bed, and this was to operate for more than a century. The sight of the tug ploughing through the tunnel (says Cromwell with mounting enthusiasm) had "a truly Tartarean aspect. The smoke, the fire, and the noise of the engine, uniting with the deep gloom of the arch, the blackness of the water, the crashing of the vessels against the sides of the tunnel and each other, and the lurid light that glimmers beyond each distant extremity, form an aggregate of infernalia . . ." [p. 126]

The canal, however, was completed too late in the day to be a commercial success, overtaken by the railways before profits could repay its capital outlay. Indeed, during the great railway age some years later, a possible transport goldmine was visualised near this reach of the New River, when incredible as it may seem, in 1867 a company was formed to build an "Essex Road Branch Railway" with one terminus behind no. 67 Colebrooke Row. From this "Islington Station" the line was to run via Packington Street and Bath Street to the City, "to terminate", according to the prospectus, "in the premises occupied as livery stables by Edmund Goddard, in Moor Lane", in St Giles's Cripplegate. Short enough in all conscience; perhaps too short, for the project soon died, although progress seems to have been made in acquiring the intervening property, and negotiating with St Luke's Workhouse over running the line through their land.

No. 67 Colebrooke Row, then occupied by Mr Frederick Jacoby, was almost at the end of old Bird's Buildings, a mid-18th century row continuing Colebrooke Row north of St Peter's Street. The proposed railway would have run east of the City Road and Wenlock canal basins, presumably ploughing through the then still newish houses of St Peter's district on the way, and continued parallel with Wenlock Street to end conveniently at or near Liverpool Street Station. But backers understandably remained backward. [Fins. Lib., map; prospectus; Central Lib., cuttings]

6) Charles Lamb

Three foot-bridges had long spanned the River, one opposite Charlton Place, another about half-way along the row, near Woodfall's, leading to Camden Street and thence to Camden Passage, and a third opposite Duncan street, by the canal exit. Over the years, the riverside footway had run successively beside pasture land, then nursery gardens and the early houses, then brickfields, often unprotected even by a railing. Crito, a correspondent writing in the *Gentleman's Magazine* in January 1799, speaks disapprovingly of the row "now building" (evidently 1–10 Duncan Terrace) because of the removal of the fence, "to the disgrace of humanity", thereby constituting a danger that on dark or foggy nights passengers might meet "a watery grave". Many an unsuspecting person did indeed fall in. One such unfortunate was the absent-minded poet George Dyer one day on leaving the house of his friend Charles Lamb.

Lamb lived from 1823 to 1827 at Colebrooke Cottage, the single house near D'Aguilar's farm that had stood alone on the north bank until New Terrace was built.

Charles Lamb's cottage, Duncan Terrace in 1851
This drawing of Colebrooke Cottage from the *Lady's Newspaper*, with the New River outside the front gate, is among the last showing the house in its original state. See Fig. 25 on p. 76

It was still free-standing, originally rated with Camden Street (whose 18th-century houses have long been demolished) and later with one or two others as "Camden Terrace".

The unmarried brother and sister Charles and Mary, both in their 50s, moved here after the domestic tragedy in which the unstable Mary in a fit of madness stabbed their mother. They now possessed the first house of their own, and here they entertained modestly the literary lions of the day; and were regarded with affection and admiration, except by the dyspeptic Thomas Carlyle, who was unfailingly vitriolic. From Colebrooke Cottage they removed to Enfield, and later to Edmonton, where Charles died, but they had an especial fondness for their first riverside home. Charles describes his acquisition to a friend:

> "a cottage, for it is detached; a white house, with six good rooms in it; the New River (rather elderly by this time) runs (if a moderate walking-pace can be so termed) close to the foot of the house; and behind is a spacious garden, with vines (I assure you) . . . You enter without passage into a cheerful dining-room . . . and above is a lightsome drawing-room, three windows . . . I feel like a great lord."

It was here that, from 1825, Charles was first able to enjoy retirement from his drudgery at the East India Office: "33 years' slavery . . . a freed man, with £441 a year for the remainder of my life".

For some time after the Lambs left, the house was empty, but was occupied from 1831 by Mr John Webb, a soda water manufacturer, who erected his factory behind the garden, later extending it as far as Islington Green (Rosoman Buildings). Like many industries of the day, this was a famous place of resort for the curious, eager to learn how manufactories operated. The business eventually removed to Lambeth (1924).

In those days Lamb's house was still detached, its entrance a storey above the river-bank, approached by a flight of steps then at right angles to the house. It has been so altered as to be almost unrecognisable, and it is difficult to see how the drawing-room could ever have accommodated three windows. Indeed, doubt has been raised over whether it was even the same house, or at least more than a gutted and re-fronted replacement over the base storey.

The Rate Books might have revealed whether there was an unoccupied period for the building in, say, the late 1870s, when major works might have been carried on, but unfortunately Rate Books have not been kept from 1860 onwards except for the decanal years. The last dated drawing of the house as Lamb knew it appears to be in the *Lady's Newspaper* of 1851, and subsequent accounts seem to be based on earlier descriptions and reveal nothing new. It is a small mystery with no foreseeable solution.

Islington Proprietary School, Duncan Terrace, and the Irvingite Church.
The church is visible behind the school on the left
From a lithograph of 1836 by W. E. Morland

7) The Churches of Duncan Terrace and Colebrooke Row

a) The Irvingite Church: When Cromwell was writing *Walks Through Islington* in 1835, two new churches had appeared within a month of each other, one on either side of the New River. Almost on the corner of Duncan Street and Duncan Terrace was the Irvingite Church, opened in November 1834, designed and built by Stevenson and Ramage of 83 Theobalds Road.

This was a temple for the egregious Scottish preacher Edward Irving (b. 1792) who after a promising debut as assistant minister to the famous Dr Chalmers in Glasgow had moved to London, where at first he drew admiring throngs of the famous with his eloquent sermons at the Hatton Garden meeting-house, and ended as centre of a cult of all-but-demented ladies speaking in tongues and convinced of the gift of prophecy. For this heresy Irving was taken to task not only by his London Presbytery but by the General Assembly of the Church of Scotland in Edinburgh, and was expelled from the body of the Kirk (1833) – to the sorrow of Thomas Carlyle, his friend from early days who in happier times had stayed with him in what is now Claremont Square, Pentonville.

Irving then took to open-air preaching, including in Britannia Fields, off the Lower Road in Islington; but his followers opened a subscription, raised £2000, and built him this small meeting-house near the New River. Within weeks of its opening on 16 November, 1834, however, Irving died in Glasgow. Cromwell, writing not long afterwards, comments drily that "it is expected that . . . the fulfilment of prophecy will be shortly seen in the gift of the *prophetical* and *apostolical* powers that distinguished the first teachers of Christianity": because according to their tenets, "the 'last days', predicted in holy writ, are arrived, or immediately at hand" – apparently interpreting as dire portents the contemporary upheavals of the 1830 French Revolution, Parliamentary and social reforms of the 1830s, and the Chartist agitation. Irving's followers shortly evolved into the Catholic Apostolic Church.

The Irvingite Church was a simple Neo-Greek building with a plain pediment and Doric pilasters, with two Ionic columns *in antis.* In 1836 it was joined at the corner of Duncan Terrace by a Proprietary School, also classical though much more elaborate, and with two wings. This was the work of John William Griffith, a surveyor and architect who acted for James Rhodes's property. He was also surveyor to the Parish of St Botolph, Aldersgate, and made alterations to the church; and surveyor to the London estates of St John's College, Cambridge. Griffith, who lived in St John's Square, Clerkenwell, died in 1855, and for nearly 40 years before that is recorded as designing villas in north London and different parts of the country. He may have been responsible for nos. 22–32 Duncan Terrace (1833–4), which were on Rhodes's land and in a more elaborate style than the terrace they adjoined. Griffith's son William Pettit Griffith was also an architect and in 1881 made the additions to no. 54 Colebrooke Row, q.v.

The Presbyterian Church, Colebrooke Row in 1952
Widford House flats are now on the site

The Irvingite church was altered out of recognition if not entirely rebuilt in 1858 by George Truefitt, and a century later, having fallen out of use, was acquired by CPO. In 1967 it was burnt out, and its site has been incorporated into the grounds of the new St John the Evangelist Primary School.

In 1851 the former Proprietary school became the Clerkenwell County Court, and served until 1929. It was then closed, moving to temporary quarters in City Road, until the present not unhandsome building was completed in 1931.

b) The Presbyterian Church: A month after the opening of the Irvingite church, a Scottish Presbyterian church was completed in River Terrace on the Colebrooke Row side. This was an even more modest affair, architect Richard Dixon, and cost only £1,250, for a congregation that since 1827 had met in Chadwell Street until their lease expired. It was a contrast both to the Neo-classic church opposite and to the surrounding houses, being in the fashionable Gothic style, with a gabled and pinnacled façade, lancet windows, buttresses and a tall 'pointed' doorway. Cromwell was succinct: "The highest praise it can aspire to is that of neatness." (p. 173) [see Lewis, 362–3] In the disruption of the Scottish Kirk in 1843 it followed the Secessionists, but as the building belonged to the established Presbyterian church, it had to be sold to the congregation: and it became an English Presbyterian Church.

With the fall in population after the First World War it lost its congregation and closed in 1923, and was subsequently used as the "Albemarle Hall", later a billiard hall, and finally a warehouse, although a stone tablet was erected in 1952 to commemorate its former identity (See (c) below).

c) Houses of the 1830s: The middle fields, held by the Rhodes family in leasehold from the Pullins, were now surrounded by the new terraces. A private Act of 1826 describes the land as "particularly eligible" for building, close to "property now in the progressive course of improvement", and empowers the trustees, who included Samuel Rhodes, to lay out streets and grant leases. Samuel's son James, a brick-maker, between 1830 and 1841 developed this central area as brickfields, and then as building land.

Lewis in 1842 describes the "several handsome ranges of houses, of modern erection, bordering on the New River, which . . . imparts to them a pleasing appearance", and praises the "good rows of buildings" which by then included the old north end of Colebrooke Row, Colebrooke or "New" Terrace (46–58 Duncan Terrace), and River Terrace (1–10 Colebrooke Row). He also notes that Duncan Terrace, begun in 1798 and in 1820 extended to no. 15, gained a further "noble continuation" in 1834 on the land of James Rhodes, and that "many large houses" — i.e. nos. 16–32 — were "in course of erection between the row and the Canal". The gaps of open space, whether nursery or brickfields, so long surviving only a minute's walk from Islington High Street, were rapidly being filled.

Even then, buildings and brickfields did not yet obscure the view from the end of the canal tunnel "as far as Hoxton and the Rosemary Branch", Cromwell tells us (p. 177). Beyond Rhodes's brickfield in the foreground, "the remains of Finsbury-fields are yet verdant . . . the prospect actually embraces five bridges over the winding canal"; though he gloomily speculates on how long this agreeable situation could continue in face of the activities of "the demons of bricks and mortar".

The demons won out fast enough. In 1837 William Watkins built River Terrace North, a short terrace of seven houses (now 13–19 Colebrooke Row) on the former Three Acres Field between two new roads, Vincent Street and Alfred (now Elia) Street. In 1838 he built two more houses, one on either side of the new Scottish church, making an extension to River Terrace North — later re-numbered 11 and 12 Colebrooke Row. In 1960 when church and flanking houses were largely derelict, the group from 6 Colebrooke Row as far as Elia Street was acquired and demolished by the LCC, and a row of 24 four-storey flats built in their place, in scale with the surrounding houses.

d) St John the Evangelist Roman Catholic Church: Latest and most architecturally distinguished of the New River-side churches was St John the Evangelist in Duncan Terrace, one of the fruits of the Catholic Emancipation Act of 1829, which freed

Catholics in England from the remaining political and social restrictions which had hampered them since the Reformation. In 1839 the Rhodes family trustees sold nearly $\frac{3}{4}$ acre, north of Duncan Street, freehold, allowing space for a school behind, and a church fronting on Duncan Terrace with a house on either side for the clergy.

The school, for boys and girls, was built first, "in the Norman style, with embattled gables". The boys' schoolroom on the ground floor served for a chapel until the new church was built in 1841–3.

St John's was designed by the noted Catholic church architect Joseph John Scoles (1798–1863), who usually favoured the Gothic style but sometimes, as here, the Norman. He had already designed the Gothic St Peter's Church (1832–5) and an observatory (1838) for Stonyhurst College, the Commissioner-like Chapel of Our lady at Grove Road, St John's Wood (1836), and, in the Norman style, St David's Church in Cardiff (1841–2). The arch-Gothicist Pugin condemned his St John the Evangelist Church as "the most original combination of modern deformity that has been erected for some time past"; while on the other hand it has been compared with the basilica of St Clement in Rome.

The church's gable end with three lancets below a rose window, and double Romanesque doorway surmounted by a large tympanum, was designed for tall flanking towers and spires. These are shown prematurely in Lewis's *History* (p. 366) with double windows set in an arch, and tall octagonal spires with corner spirelets, but lack of funds delayed the church's completion. Its side chapels long remained unfinished, and not until 1873 was work begun on the towers.

These were designed by another well-known Catholic architect, Francis William Tasker (1848–1906), whose recent works had included St Charles College, Paddington (1872–4), with an unusual tower, and St Joseph's Retreat on Highgate Hill (1875). St John the Evangelist's towers differed not only from Scoles's original but also from each other. Both have slender engaged columns at the corners with plain cushion capitals; the south tower is low with a cap spire and single windows on each side; the taller northern tower has a broach spire, double windows, blind arcade and machicolation. They even convey a faint whiff of those French cathedrals whose spires contrast because of different dates – whereas here they are contemporary, and deliberately different. The top stage of the south tower, and the two spires, were completed only in 1877.

The spacious interior is (as Pevsner puts it) "somewhat bleak and barn-like", aisleless, with arched openings to side chapels and confessionals, and an apsidal altar end whose frescoes by Edward Armitage have been painted over, and its windows blocked up. Side lighting is entirely from clerestory windows, the church being shut in by houses on either side. The enclosed site not only confined all external features to the eastern façade, but dictated that the liturgical position was reversed, the high altar being necessarily at the west end.

St John the Evangelist Roman Catholic Church, Duncan Terrace in 1953.
Showing the gap where no. 34 was destroyed in World War II

Tasker also remodelled the original tie-beam trusses in 1901 to produce the present hammerbeam roof. Other changes were made in the 1950s and 1960s, and in 1977–8 a youth centre was created by excavating and adapting the crypt, by the architect Joan Davis. (Isl. Chapels 57–60; Pevsner; Colvin 723–4).

Rebuilding planned for the adjoining priest's house, no. 39, in a style matching the church, was never executed; for which – for the sake of the symmetry of the terrace – we may perhaps be grateful.

A leading figure in St John the Evangelist's early days was the Revd Frederick Oakeley (1802–80), Tractarian and follower of Newman, and from 1852 a Canon of Westminster Cathedral; in 1850 he was appointed missionary Rector of St John's, where he served until his death. He was known as a friend to the many poor Irish immigrants living in the Angel and City Road area, for whom the church was a centre. Canon Oakeley died in 1880 at 39 Duncan Terrace.

8) The last houses

The building of St John's Church coincided with infilling of the last major gaps on either side of the New River. These terraces, built in 1841 by William Watkins, strongly resemble each other. First came nos. 34–39 Duncan Terrace, as "New Duncan Terrace", followed shortly afterwards by the balancing row north of the church (40–45). Nos. 39 and 40, built for church use, were later occupied by the Sisters of the Holy Cross and their school for young ladies; no. 42 was acquired in 1902 as a Home for Catholic Working Girls in London. No. 36 was destroyed in the Second World War, and subsequently rebuilt in facsimile. Watkins also built Montagu Place, 11 houses on the opposite side of the river between the canal and Gerrard Road, and a single house north of Gerrard Road. These were renumbered (1864) as 20–31 Colebrooke Row; nos. 29, 30 and 31 have been demolished.

Lamb's Cottage, until well on in the century, was still framed in an almost rural setting, but at last linked with Duncan Terrace in 1880, when three inharmoniously tall, gaunt Victorian houses (nos. 61–63) joined it with what had been the short Camden Terrace, with which it had been included for rating purposes. Two of these houses, later renumbered 59 and 60 Duncan Terrace, were demolished for the building in 1969 of the Council's Colinsdale, a series of flats extending from Camden Passage down Camden Street, now pedestrianised and re-named Camden Walk.

The terraces retained their individual names for many years. In 1864 the east side of the river, including River Terrace, River Terrace North and Montagu Place was 'rationalised' and re-numbered as Colebrooke Row.

West of the river was re-named Duncan Terrace only in 1890, incorporating Duncan Terrace, New Duncan Terrace, New Terrace, and Camden Terrace.

9) Later History

Towards the end of the 19th century the two streets suffered the common fate of Islington, falling into industrial and commercial use and then generally decaying. For example, in 1932 no. 41 Colebrooke Row, a 10-roomed house with no bathroom, already in multi-occupation for light industry, was offered for sale with the inducement of a long back garden considered suitable for a rear factory extension. Several were demolished over the years, chiefly since the last war. One of the earliest depredations was the loss of nos. 37–40 in 1914, for the building of the LCC Colebrooke School for Mentally Defective Children, set in the usual yard behind a high brick wall. In 1951 it became a school for ESN Senior Girls, and is now an all-age school for mentally handicapped children. After the 1950s the fine houses began by degrees to be salvaged and restored, though many are still used for offices or industry.

The New River disappeared in 1861, first enclosed in a pipe and the river-bed dug out, and at length covered up and planted with shrubs and flowers. In 1950 even the pipe was removed, for by then the river had been terminated some miles north at Stoke Newington. The former river-bed was designated one of a score of open spaces planned for post-war improvement by the Borough Council: ownership of the site was transferred in 1951, and in 1952 it was laid out anew as gardens, attractively at the City Road end, though farther north the much narrower space is not greatly enhanced by the scattering of incongruous Westmorland rocks.

In time the roadway itself came under threat, first in the late 1950s when the Council proposed to widen the 'bottleneck' at the junction with St Peter's Street, a threatened barbarism which lingered on amid opposition until finally dropped in 1967. Soon afterwards, however, there was an attempt to erode the other end when the GLC's massive Angel road-widening and underpass scheme was a dreaded possibility, and both Duncan Terrace and Colebrooke Row were expected to be closed at the City Road. One weekend in 1971 residents awoke to the sound of part of the gardens being dug up to make space for a 'slip road', like some monstrous colostomy bypassing the exit. The Council yielded to protests, and instead only Duncan Terrace was closed, and the slip road converted into a short turning bay at the end of what is now a cul-de-sac.

Erosion of the original buildings over the last few decades, and replacement by not always happy Council building – to which Colinsdale is a notable exception – have not destroyed the atmosphere and quality of the long and dignified terraces that once bordered a reach of the New River. Could the water only be returned to its original bed, how much enhanced one of Islington's most noble streets would be.

ARCHITECTURE

Except where otherwise stated, all houses are of three storeys with attic and basement.

56–59

This picturesque group, the oldest in the row, are also among Islington's oldest surviving houses. The difficulty is to date them. Nos. 56 and 57, an obvious pair, of only two storeys and attics in pitched roofs, may be survivals of the houses built by Walter Burton in or after 1717 connected with his brew-house and kilns; No. 57 seems to have been the Castle Inn. They have linked door-heads, cantilevered and hooded, carried on brackets, and flush windows under segmental heads. Although the fronts are at the same level, the windows of No. 57 are slightly above those of its pair. The interiors contain original deal panelling, cupboards and staircases. No. 57, restored for himself in 1952 by Walter Ison, architect and author of books on Georgian Bath and Bristol, was occupied in the late 1950s and 1960s by Cyril Ray, the journalist and connoisseur of food and wine.

Nos. 58 and 59, facing down the street and externally somewhat Victorianised, originally stood free of the others, and were knocked into one when used as a school by the Rev. Mr Rule. About 1795 they were separated again, and the exteriors much altered. In the 19th century No. 58 was enlarged and joined to No. 57 by a shallow L-shaped extension, now Nos. 57a and 58a, including a rather awkwardly rearranged front entrance (58a), stucco ground floor, and segmental upper window-heads. No. 58, stuccoed throughout, evidently had its windows renewed in the later 18th century; the low-rise No. 59 was refronted, and also acquired a flat western wall concealing its double-pitched roof, with new Victorian windows, placed asymmetrically and opening on its small yard in the angle with St Peter's Street.

54, 55 (c. 1745, 1755)

Two houses built at different dates by Samuel Steemson, carpenter, after he leased part of Tile Kiln Field; they were sold with the rest of the property about 1775 to William Cross, whose executors held it some 10 years later. Dating is difficult because of conflicting details in the early leases.

No. 55, a 5-bay house, is now lopsided through the substitution on the upper floors of single Victorian windows for two of the originals. Similarly, the large rectangular porch is not quite central.

Between two of the 2nd-floor windows a faded sign reads "Women only 9d and 1/— per night. 4/6 and 6/— per week." The puzzle is to what date this relates, as directories show no such use. In 1896 it was run as a home for Catholic youths and from 1906 for many years was kept by Mr David Levey as a lodging-house, though the directories never indicate that this might be solely for women. From 1918 it was in industrial use.

The taller, flat-fronted No. 54 was much restored in the 1980s, with a raised attic and 're-Georgianised' facsimile windows, reversing the Victorianisation carried out

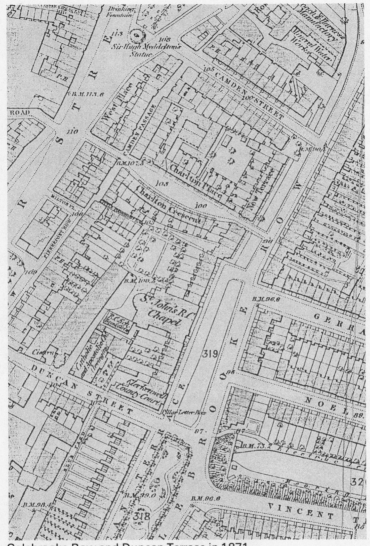

Colebrooke Row and Duncan Terrace in 1871
The New River is already filled in; the Victorian houses adjoining Lamb's
Cottage are not yet built

in 1881 by William Pettit Griffith, who inserted two florid bay windows and added an elaborate porch, all now removed. The house stands just free of No. 53.

34–36 & 41–53 (1768 and c. 1772–4)

The original Colebrooke Row. Three-bay façades unadorned apart from handsome pedimented doorcases with varied capitals, and a 3-row brick band above the first floor. Nos. 47–53 were built within a short time by Josiah Collins (see p. 57); the next houses, 34–46, in the same style under the ownership of Richard Masefield, c. 1772–4 after Collins's bankruptcy.

All windows are rectangular, lintels picked out in red brick. Most attics have been renewed, and Nos. 47, 49 and 50 raised by a storey. Nos. 43–48 and 51–53 have lost their astragals. No. 45 has a different doorway, under a brick arch with impost blocks, 46 a tall rectangular doorhead with bracket, and 50 even taller but flat, 51 a plain rectangular doorcase.

Nos. 37–40 were destroyed, leaving a jagged end, for the building of Colebrooke School (1914), set back behind a high-walled playground (see p. 70).

No. 36 belongs in style to the previous group. No. 35 is grander, with engaged columns and plaster ovals, roundels and entablature. First-floor windows have alternating segmental/pedimented/segmental entablatures and brackets; ground-floor windows are similar to No. 34 but with plain entablatures. No. 34, also with neo-classic detail, has only two bays, a smaller house evidently to fill the remaining space at the end of Collins's plot, next to a narrow entry. A single late Victorian window has unfortunately replaced the original on the ground floor.

No. 32 (bearing the datestone) and 33 were destroyed along with Woodfall's cottage (see p. 57), together with William Watkins's No. 31 (see p. 74), and replaced by Hermitage House (1959), a singularly graceless block with metal windows and pebble-dash, its ground-floor windows rendered off-white.

20–23, 24–28 (= Montagu Place) (1841)

These terraces are William Watkins's, filling in the last gaps on either side of Noel Road, not unlike Roumieu and Gough's work (see Milner Square). Ground and top floor windows of all houses are round-headed, the top windows inset in arcades, and a moulded cornice below the top floor. They were crowned by another low cornice, but this has vanished except on Nos. 23 and 25.

Nos. 20–23, a mansion-like block, resembled paired villas, Nos. 21 and 22 slightly advanced. Ground floors in rusticated stucco, with continuous balcony above.

The terraces are not identical, and Nos. 24–28 north of Noel Road, now lacking the original Nos. 29 and 30, had three central houses and two flanking, instead of two and one. No. 20 has a porch extension with balustrade above, while 23 and 24 have side entrances in Noel Road; most end wall windows (in No. 23 all) are blank. The northern terrace has continuous first-floor balconies of different design, and its

The New River and Colebrooke Row in 1825
Woodfall's cottage is on the right.
From a water-colour by C. Barrow

ground-floor windows are set lower, with longer keystones over the front doors. Nos. 25–27 retain circle-and-teardrop fanlights. The 2nd floor has elaborate window-guards.

Originally this northern group had two more houses (Nos. 29 and 30), and Watkins built one more, No. 31, north of Gerrard Road. Nos. 29 and 30 have been rebuilt as Asman House (1963), with entrances in Gerrard Road: innocuous pastiche, except that nowhere does it match its neighbours – typical 1960s lack of architectural manners in Council rebuilding, though not as bad as Hermitage House.

13–19 (= River Terrace North) (1837)

William Watkins's earlier contribution occupies the space between Elia Street and Vincent Terrace, in which the end houses, Nos. 13 and 19, have their entrances. The row, four floors with basements, shows nice variation: stuccoed ground floor in simulated ashlar (unusual in Islington) with a cill band above, a narrower band below the 2nd floor, and moulded cornice below the top floor. The end houses, slightly advanced, are distinguished by quoins, with single three-light ground-floor windows under a bracketed head (No. 19 still has its rosettes), and round-headed first-floor windows. The central house, No. 16, is similar; the rest reverse the round-headed and rectangular arrangement. Mouldings at door-head level link the ground floors of 14–18 like an arcade, with rusticated window surround, and except for No. 16 the circular-headed doors are paired.

1–5 with 389 City Road (River Terrace) (1798–9 and 1808, 1814) and Widford House (1966)

The original terrace, of which only six houses survive, was built over a period of 40 years. The remaining few present a problem of conflicting evidence: Dent's 1806 map shows three only, as "Duncan Place", slightly away from the City Road corner, whereas in the 1798–9 rate-books four are identifiable. They were re-named "River Terrace" in 1808, when two were added, and included 389 City Road. Four more houses were added in 1814, but all these later houses except Nos. 4 and 5 have been demolished along with the Presbyterian church of 1834 and William Watkins's two houses built one on either side of it in 1838 (Nos. 11 and 12). Their GLC replacement, Widford House (1966), is a pleasant series of 24 flats, alternating advanced fronts with recessed patios, and recessed fronts with advanced brick balconies.

No. 389 City Road is slightly advanced, as the end of a terrace, with grooved stucco ground floor and mansard attics. All balconies are continuous up to No. 3, all ground-floor windows round-headed, the narrow fronts accommodating two. Nos. 1–3 retain fanlights of three interlocked circles.

The slight change of style is visible in the later Nos. 4 and 5, with longer, 9-light drawing-room sashes set in blank recesses, and a narrow cill band below. No. 5 has a rayed half-circle fanlight.

Duncan Terrace

Colebrooke Cottage, No.64

This at least in part the oldest building on this side, perhaps about 1760, and until 1981 the only building beyond it was the semi-derelict garage-workshop on part of the site of "Starvation Farm". Restoration in the 1970s revealed evidence of its old side windows from before the adjoining No. 63 was built (*c.* 1880). The house now has an early Victorian look, and has been endowed – apparently in 1879 – with keystones and window surrounds, and its entrance stair straightened. It bears only a general resemblance to views of it taken in 1851 and thereabouts and to Lamb's description, including his "three fine windows" in the drawing-room. There are now only two (and how could the small frontage have accommodated more?). It has even been claimed that this not the original cottage at all, though for this there is no evidence, and one can only conclude that the Victorian renovation was more thorough than one would have liked.

61–63 (?1880)

These three Victorian houses linked Colebrooke Cottage with the early "Camden Terrace", whose few houses were demolished for the building in 1969 of the

Colebrooke Cottage in 1907
By now the New River is covered in, a Victorian terrace has been built
alongside, industrial buildings have encroached and the house itself is altered
almost out of recognition

Council's Colinsdale, a well-designed small estate stretching from Camden Passage, the Duncan Terrace front unobtrusive and set flush with the row. Camden Street, now re-named Camden Walk was re-routed, narrowed and pedestrianised at the same time. Nos. 61–63 are $3\frac{1}{2}$ storeys, the half being a semi-basement, and the 'ground' floor level with that of Colebrooke Cottage, similarly reached by steep flights of steps. The splayed, polygonal window-heads, plate glass and keystones look incongruous in this predominantly classical street.

The road here is narrow, with space only for a grassy verge and a few of the Westmorland boulders which represent the course of the New River.

50–58 (New Terrace) (1791), and 46–49 (1793)

James Taylor built the first complete terrace on the west bank of the New River, nine houses set back on a high pavement, styled "New Terrace 1791" on a plaque above No. 54. At the same time he built his Charlton Place and Crescent (1790 and 1791), and in 1793 the associated terrace just beyond (Nos. 46–49).

New Terrace creates its effect by elegant simplicity – perfectly plain but for thin mouldings marking the tops of end and centre houses. Only the ground-floor windows are round-headed; the tall drawing-room windows have cill bands below, and except for No. 54 with its decorated balconies they have only three fender-like bars. The most elaborate feature is the front doors, with Coade-stone masks as keystones, and moulded imposts. Most houses retain their shutters, and all their lamp-holders; fanlights are mostly cobwebby, with swags, and the railings elaborate, lozengy.

The front doors of Nos. 50 and 49 face one another across Charlton Place, No. 50 the grander, with flattened bows, a cill band below first floor and blank windows above the door. No. 49, similarly up steps, has a wide door with elaborate fanlight – actually fan-shaped – with one window above on each floor, and set between slightly advanced blocks as on the front façade, with all blank windows above.

Nos. 46–49 have a rustic stucco ground floor, the end houses with one bay very advanced, like 'pavilion' ends, and top windows within an arched recess. Like New Terrace, ground-floor windows are round-headed, but inset in lengthened embrasures – somewhat like the considerably later Wilmington Square. Drawing-room windows are tall with a narrow cill band below; a few graceful balconies survive.

The front door of No. 46, in a set-back extension of the return wall with blank windows above, presumably indicates an infill of space left when the next terrace was built. Nos. 46 and 47 were for many years occupied by a monastic foundation and combined into one, connected laterally by through corridors, and with a chapel on the ground floor. A 1992 conversion restored the buildings to separate houses, with the front door of No. 47, which had been turned into a window, reinstated.

34–39 and 40–45 (1841)

This matching pair of terraces, set well back from their neighbours, was built to flank St John the Evangelist Church; and they reflect Nos. 24–28 Colebrooke Row opposite, except that their stuccoing is the more usual grooved version, and their top windows are not set in arches. Only the end houses (34/39, 40/45) are set back from the rest. The southern group, 34–39, has simplified Gothicky astragals (except 39) and circle-and-teardrop fanlights – except 34, which is in fact a post-war facsimile of the original destroyed in the war, otherwise indistinguishable externally except for its lighter brick (and air-brick inserts) and slightly 'wrong'-shaped fanlight.

Nos. 39 and 40, immediately adjoining the church, were built for its clergy. No. 40's first-floor windows have been altered, presumably early this century. This range, 40–45, has plate-glass fanlights.

At the corner of Duncan Street the red-brick Clerkenwell Court, rebuilt in 1930–31, occupies the site of the Proprietary School (see p. 65).

16–32 (1829; 1833/4)

Although these houses form a continuous row with Nos. 2–15, their history is quite different, being the Rhodes family's earliest venture into the house-building market, but it got off to a slow start, and there seems then to have been a change of plan. The architect was presumably John W. Griffith, who applied to the Commissioners of Sewers in 1828 for drainage of 18 houses he was about to build, submitting a plan in 1829, but the leases date only from 1833/4, when the houses were still empty. Frank Kelsall suggests that James Rhodes may have had a lease proper on only part of the site and an agreement on the rest. The boundary house was No. 22, whose two halves had to be separately leased to the builder. The actual builder of Nos. 22–32 was James Hambber; no name is recorded for Nos. 16–21.

There are in fact 17 houses, of which No. 22 serves as both termination of the first 'terrace' and first of the next, although stylistically it belongs to the later group ending at No. 32. Both groups have fully rusticated stucco on the ground floor – relatively rare in Islington.

16–21: ground floor rusticated stucco, with heavy cill band above, and circular features; balustraded top. First-floor windows in 'New River' style, rectangular windows in sunk panels, and single window-guards or balconies of the Gibson Square variety, lacy anthemion and curlicues. No.16, which alone has lost its fanlight, has small circular-headed top-floor windows, and a front-door extension with two storeys above. Nos. 19–21 have mansard attics.

Nos. 22–32, rather more elaborate in detail, have a rhythm 1–3–(3)–3–1, the middle three (Nos. 25–28) advanced; continuous anthemion balconies, and mansard attics. No. 22 alone has a balustrade instead of cornice, and round-headed ground-floor windows – the rest have rectangular. Doorways are wider, with engaged columns and elaborate fanlights, of which Nos. 24–26, 28, 31 and 32 still retain their original inset lanterns.

2–10 (?1798–1803); 11–14 (c. 1820); 15

This group is outwith the Rhodes development. No. 1 has long been demolished, replaced by a 1950s building in the City Road. The houses are similar to 1–3 Colebrooke Row opposite, but in Nos. 2–5 doors and ground-floor windows are recessed in red-brick arches, and the houses are 3-bay throughout (as 389 City Road). Nos. 8–14 balance the other six, reversing front doors and windows. Tall, 4–pane drawing-room windows; fanlights mostly cobweb style, 11 and 12 with elaborate geometrical variation. No. 5 has a Coade keystone grotesque. Most retain their shutters, and 6 and 7 their lamp-holders. Balconies and window-guards of various patterns, though 5 and 7 have lost theirs.

Nos. 11–14, which completed the group about 1820, are more in New River style: first-floor windows in recessed arches, with string-courses. The astragals of 12–14 are clumsy straight cut. No. 15 looks like an infill, very plain, with single windows and a narrow door wedged against the party wall; no attic.

No. 4, now derelict, but under negotiation for restoration, displays an old LCC plaque erected to Edward Suess (1831–1914), economist and statesman, who was born here.

Compton Terrace (1805–9, 1819–31) (see Canonbury Square)

In 1819 Compton Terrace consisted only of the chapel flanked by a pair of houses on either side, from the first building period by Henry Leroux (see *Canonbury Square*). When building eventually resumed the terrace was to be completed as a continuous row. In 1819 and 1822 Lord Northampton (now a Marquess) signed standard agreements with Henry Flower, a builder in Clerkenwell, and Samuel Kell, carpenter and builder of Red Lion Street, Holborn, for building the rest of the terrace, both north and south of the chapel, within three years. It was to be substantial, of good materials, "in a regular uniform elevation . . . corresponding with the houses already built"; by Flower and Kell; and at least 14 houses, 2nd-rate, of three storeys, with coach-houses and stables, and "greenhouses or summerhouses" at the ends of the gardens.

Fourteen leases were granted in 1821, then no more until 1827; by 1831, 12 more had been granted. In all 37 houses were built. (The north end was damaged by bombing in the Second World War, and the terrace now ends at no. 25.)

This nearly 30-year project was a slow beginning to what was to become a flood of building. Kell died early in the proceedings, and in 1823, when nine houses had been built north of the chapel, the then lessees, who were Flower, Kell's executors,

Compton Terrace in the 1960s
The two houses on the left were demolished for enlargement of Highbury
Corner in 1966

and some half-dozen others, by agreement made a private road in front of the houses, with "a paddock or grassplot" as a "pleasure ground", enclosed by "a dwarf wall and iron fence with gates". Here no clothes-drying was allowed, nor storage of "Timber, Stone, bricks, lime or any other material whatsoever". The occupiers, forming a committee of management, were to share the costs of planting and maintaining the trees and gardens. Samuel Lewis speaks approvingly of the "plantation" secluding the houses from the high road. (p. 170).

Architecture
Only 25 of the 37 houses of Compton Terrace remain: the northernmost were destroyed or seriously damaged when a V2 hit the Highbury Corner area in 1944 with great loss of life, and the rest were demolished for the enlarging of Highbury Corner in 1966. The north end is banked up where there is a slight fall in ground level.

The four houses of 1806, by Henry Leroux, are nos. 17–20 on either side of the chapel, built as paired villas with recessed two-bay front-door extensions. The extensions, originally single-storey, were later raised (no. 17 to three floors) except for no. 20 which alone retains its original proportions. Nos. 17 and 20 have handsome doorcases and a plain sunk panel above the adjoining window; 18's extension is extremely narrow. The second bay of both 18 and 19 was lost when the present Union Chapel was built.

These four houses are of 3 floors and basement, two also with attics. The ground-floor windows are round-headed; drawing-room floor windows extend to floor level as in Canonbury Square N side (those at 19 have later been reduced), with a broad cill band.

The rest of the terrace, nos. 1–16 of 1819–21 and 21–25 of 1827–31, are by Henry Flower and Samuel Kell. The complete terrace was always slightly asymmetrical, with 18 houses south of the chapel and 19 north of it (now 12), although the southern terrace has wider frontages.

Nos. 1–16 are of 3 storeys and basements, though some have had mansard attics added, e.g. 12, 13. Features (except fanlights) are now rectangular and drawing-rooms shorter. Also a broad cill band, and single window-guards, with Gothicky detail. No. 12 has a later, rather clumsy stuccoed ground floor; in several, astragals have given way to plate glass, especially on the ground floors and at the S end.

No. 7 has a cast-iron Victorian porch; 1 and 5 Ionic porticos – 1 in an extended entrance block; while 3 evidently once had one, retaining its rectangular door-case framed with stucco rosettes, and the stumps of *fluted* columns. No. 1, the corner house, has additional windows on the end wall.

Nos. 21–25 are grander, 4 floors and basement, first-floor full balconies with anthemion detail. Nos. 21, 22 have rusticated stucco ground floors, 23–25 plain grooved stucco.

Despite the truncation by bomb damage, Compton Terrace remains one of the area's best preserved and most dignified terraces.

Inhabitants
At no. 13 in 1882 lived John Betjeman, grandfather of Sir John the Poet Laureate.

At no. 19 lived the Samuel Lewises, father and son; the elder, a publisher, died here in 1865; his son the younger Samuel, author of *The History, Topography and Antiquities of the Parish of St Mary Islington* (1842), had lived at 28 Highbury Place, and was later at Priory Villas (Canonbury Park South), where he died in 1862.

At no. 25 from 1952–7 lived the Rev. Joost de Blank, who became Archbishop of Cape Town in 1957. Earlier it had been the home of the Rt Rev. R. Hamilton Moberley and his wife when he was Bishop of Stepney (1938–52).

Union Chapel (1876–7; tower 1889)
In 1799 an evangelical group of Anglican and Non-conformist worshippers began meeting independently at a small chapel at no. 18 Highbury Grove, adopting the name Union Chapel to symbolise catholicity of both services and preachers – the precursor of the Congregational movement. In 1806 they built a permanent chapel

The first Union Chapel in 1820
with two of the original houses on either side
from a contemporary engraving

nearer Islington, as central feature of Henry Leroux's new Compton Terrace: a 5-bay Palladian frontage with pedimented and pilastered centre-piece on a rusticated base, and crowned with a cupola. The chapel was considerably altered in 1839 by addition of an imposing Ionic temple portico with a heavy entablature, and a neo-Greek lantern above.

From 1804 the minister was the Rev. Thomas Lewis, who died in 1852 after 48 years' service, and was succeeded by his co-pastor the Rev. Henry Allon, under whom the congregation expanded dramatically until his death 40 years later. In 1847 the chapel joined the Congregational Union.

Allon's success as a preacher drew large numbers of the rapidly growing population, and the chapel became so famous that it was enlarged in 1859/61, but by the 1870s a new building had become necessary.

The large, robust red-brick chapel with stone dressings now designed by the architect James Cubitt transformed Compton Terrace, overflowing on to the gardens of the adjoining houses (nos. 18 and 19). Its foundation was laid on 16 May 1876 on the site of the old building, and until its completion only 18 months later the congregation was served by the usual Victorian stopgap of a temporary iron church, in Highbury, alternating with Myddelton Hall in Almeida Street.

The new chapel, built by L. H. & R. Roberts and costing in total about £50,000, was formally opened on 5 December 1877, with the Bishop of Birmingham as preacher, and Mr W. E. Gladstone, who was a friend of the minister's, among the numerous congregation. The building was designed to hold 1,800, though during its first fortnight of existence it was claimed that the celebrated Rev. C. H. Spurgeon preached to a congregation of 3,365. In 1889 the fabric was completed by the addition of the huge, sturdy pinnacled and gabled tower on its main front.

A fine organ by Father Willis – builder of the organ at the Albert Hall – was installed. The Rev. Henry Allon, a gifted preacher and a practical Christian, was also a great music-lover, and during his incumbency built up the service to a level of renowned musical performance, reviving old tunes and introducing chorales and hymns from Germany and France. The effect of the huge organ, combined with well over 1000 singers in the congregation, was powerful. Many organists visited from distant places in order to play on it.

Allon served twice as President of the Congregational Union, and travelled extensively in the USA; he was made a Doctor of Divinity at Yale in 1871, when his chapel was at the height of its fame. At the time of his death, however, the congregation was declining in numbers because of the fashionable emigration to outer suburbs.

The trend continued, and during the 2nd World War the Rev. Ronald Taylor, appointed minister in 1940 and like Henry Allon serving for 40 years, had to contend with bomb damage, a decaying building and dwindling numbers. Shortly after his death the chapel, in a bad state of repair and its congregation fallen to about a dozen, was threatened with demolition, but a proposal in 1981 to replace it with a pastiche of its small classical predecessor met with a storm of protest.

National amenity societies were called in, in 1982 a group of Friends of Union Chapel was formed as a registered charity, demolition plans were halted and alternative uses discussed. In 1984 an initial grant from the Historic Buildings Commission helped to finance roof and dry rot repairs. Since then further extensive restoration has been undertaken with an English Heritage grant, and – continuing the chapel's musical tradition – extended use has been found by letting to recording companies, concerts and music festivals (such as the Almeida) and small theatre companies, for which the excellent acoustics make the building especially suitable.

Union Chapel is now a Grade II* listed building, and with good publicity has become well known. Since 1986, under the Rev. Janet Wootton as minister, the congregation has again begun to increase.

In 1988 a silver clock, presented to the Rev. Thomas Lewis in 1839, was entered for sale by a descendent and was bought by Koopman's for £11,000. The clock, with a movement by B. L. Vulliamy, in an elaborate rococo-style case by Benjamin Smith, and surmounted by an open book surrounded by a sunburst, is on a stand bearing a presentation inscription.

James Cubitt's Union Chapel
As drawn by the architect in 1889

Architecture

Union Chapel, hailed as among the most remarkable of Victorian churches, was also outstanding among non-conformist chapels in adapting the Gothic to contemporary needs. It resembles Cubitt's design for a model church in his *Church Designs for Congregations* (1870), and his slightly later Church of the Redeemer at Edgbaston, Birmingham (unfortunately demolished in 1975). Based on the church of Santa Fosca at Torcello, it consists of a vast irregular octagon within a Greek cross — a remarkable marriage of the two forms by galleries and arcades, providing maximum sightlines despite the numerous pillars. The arches of the triple arcade carrying the gallery on N and S are barely pointed, while those of E and W are steeply 'Early English'; surmounting the four shorter sides is a segmental arch, repeated as a pendentive just below roof level.

The top-lit octagonal timber roof is also irregularly proportioned, though less so than the space it spans. The transition is subtly if not altogether successfully achieved (as appears from the width of the blind triple arcade in the segments) by the spandrels across the shorter sides.

The whole effect is of enormous depth and soaring height, enhanced by the numerous broad lancets eccentrically placed at different levels and in the angles. From any part of the steeply raked galleries the view is uninterrupted — as Cubitt intended — and equally impressive.

Immediately in front of the gallery runs a continuous band of polished 'tiles' in variegated coloured marbles. Above the vestry door, mounted in a cusped niche, is a fragment of the 'Plymouth rock' on which the Pilgrim Fathers landed in Massachusetts in December, 1620. It was presented in 1883 at Allon's request by the Pilgrim Society of America. Allon himself is commemorated in a stained glass window in the S gallery, by Lavers and Westlake.

The great organ by Father Willis was installed behind the lofty, almost Islamic pulpit, and concealed behind a triple ironwork screen across the East arcade. Another, Romanesque arcade surmounts this at gallery level. The organ still retains the two hydraulic pumps by which it was originally worked, though since 1926 it has run by electric motor. Otherwise, apart from one stop replaced in 1909, it is as Henry Willis built it.

At the rear of the building a large galleried hall, capable of holding 1,000 children, was formerly used for many years as a Sunday school.

The Tower: The robust brick tower with stone dressings, almost too stout for the church itself, has a massive double entrance framed in a lofty arch with a gable above, extending to the second stage of blind lancets, bounded by a string course. In the high, relatively bare next stage, triple lancets with blind roundels above are surmounted by a large bracket clock. At the top, double unglazed openings enclosed in an arch marry ill with the steep gabled arcade, and spirelet crowning all. The tower is visible from the most unexpected angles and distances.

Cornwallis Square (1988-90)

In the early 19th century ten acres of arable land, a little off the Holloway Road and north of the present Tollington Way, were owned by Mr John Harman and leased to John Thompson. Some 40 years later, the then owner being Mr James Peachey, it was still a 9-acre field, plus an acre turned over to allotments. With the pressure for ever new suburbs in the 1860s, a series of terraces was built on the land, partly called Cornwallis Road, and opposite these in 1865 seven acres were acquired by the West London Union Workhouse as a new site.

This was a step forward in workhouse history, with the tardy realisation that the sick poor needed special accommodation as distinct from the 'merely' poor. The stigma remained, but at least from the latter part of the century the most unfortunate members of society were not herded indiscriminately together, old, sick and able-bodied though destitute.

The building then erected stood for 120 years, having been taken over for the Islington Parish Workhouse in 1887; and when that was amalgamated with a newer workhouse at St John's Way (itself demolished 1972), during the First World War it was temporarily used as an internment camp. It later became a GPO Postal Order office and Telecommunications workshop and store, and finally closed in 1986, when under the Borough Development Plan the site was allotted to housing and open space.

There is an irony about certain developments which we may interpret as we will. On this site where for many decades in the past some of society's unhappiest and most deprived members had sunk for shelter, a new and imaginative housing scheme was now devised for members on their hopeful way up.

The old building was demolished to make way for mixed flats and town houses of varying sizes, by Countryside Properties in association with the New Islington and Hackney Housing Association, Circle 33 Housing Trust, and St George's Housing Association. In the first phase (1988) 108 units were built, of which nearly half were sold within weeks, at prices ranging from £80,000 for one-bedroom flats and £160,000 for 3-bedroom houses. The project cost some £10 million. When complete it formed 188 units of houses and flats, some designed for handicapped residents, others offered at a reduced rate for young couples.

The accommodation was available to both council and housing association tenants. The object was to rejuvenate neglected and derelict sites by building an estate which brought house ownership to a wider public. Widely advertised as "Rebirth of the Classic Square", much was made of such traditional features as balconies, full-length casement windows, and (for some) 'Adam'-style fireplaces, panelled doors and so forth. In 1989 it won first prize in the "What House?" awards for Best Urban Renewal.

The landscaped estate adapts the form of a square with central gardens – but, unconsciously echoing an old Islington tradition, with the omission of one side, in this case the east, abutting on the main road. The style is a blend of developer's housing and pastiche classical. There are ill-placed pediments, little triangular bays, tripartite windows, the odd gablet and oeil-de-boeuf, railings and window-guards scattered about the façades. At least the intention was good and the environment well chosen. Good marks for trying.

Edward Square (1853)

A humble little square, long vanished but still commemorated by a street sign, although nothing remains but a broad, unkempt stretch of grass behind the Caledonian Road.

The square was begun in 1853, when 10 houses were "newly erected", and completed by 1860 with 53 houses, the owner being a Mrs Rhodes. The layout was asymmetrical, 15 houses on the west side, only eight on the north, and the rest ranged irregularly round the other sides; and it was not built on the highway but tucked behind, reached by an alley through Edward Terrace, a component block of the Caledonian Road. Its appearance may be gauged from the part of Edward Terrace still surviving, from the corner of Copenhagen Street to the north side of the alley, although these have been converted to shops. The range south of the small passage, except for the "Little Prince of Wales" pub, has been rebuilt as W. H. Smith Garages.

At the SW corner a passage led to the Copenhagen School (renamed 1937 and several times reorganised and merged, from a foundation originally opened in 1874). On the south side, houses looked on to the canal, but this view was subsequently cut off by the building of new flats.

Edward Square, in a poor part of Islington, seems to have made no mark on history. It was chiefly occupied by families, with few commercial occupiers (for example in 1888, no. 53 was a dyers', Peter A. Higgins & Co.). The area was damaged in the Second World War, left as a bomb-site and dump for outsize junk, and used as a car-breaker's yard, to the great annoyance of remaining residents. By 1963 it was considered in such bad condition that an LCC medical officer told a Public Inquiry that "all the properties . . . are unfit for human habitation, and unreclaimable". The 84 remaining families were accordingly rehoused, and in 1964/5 the square was demolished – after which the site was invaded by rabbit-sized rats, possibly from an old sewer.

The central garden had been taken over by the Vestry as early as 1890 under an Open Spaces Act of 1887; it was let to the Metropolitan Public Gardens Association, and opened for public access in 1888 by their Chairman, the Earl of Meath.

After demolition of the houses, the cleared side was intended for new Catholic schools. In 1969, however, the Council applied to the magistrates' court for closure

Edward Square in 1950
The low-rise square was demolished in the 1960s and only the grassed central
area survives

from the rear boundaries of 157 and 159 Caledonian Road, and pending building of
the schools the GLC 'temporarily' laid out the now cleared area in grass for games
purposes. Meanwhile, however, Islington's school population was steadily falling,
and Edward Square remains as grassed space to this day. In the late 1980s the London
Wildlife Trust pointed out that as an open space it was all but derelict, and if planted
with trees and used more imaginatively could contribute greatly to the environment.
Trees have been planted on an extension to Copenhagen Street; otherwise there has
been no change to date – save for the completion in 1992 of a neat bijou 'mews'-type
flat development at the end of the passage from Caledonian Road.

An oddity of the square site is that the back gardens of Edward Terrace, along the
main road, are much lower than the present open space – presumably due to a rise in
level when the houses were demolished.

Gibson Square (1831 & 1836–9) and the Milner-Gibson Estate

East of the Back Road and parallel with the Cloudesley estate an irregularly shaped
piece of land was held of the Tufnells, Lords of the Manor of Barnsbury, by the

Milner-Gibson family, who owned property at Theberton in Suffolk. Their fortune came from plantations in Trinidad. Major Thomas Milner-Gibson died in 1807, leaving a son, also Thomas, born in Trinidad only a year earlier. This Thomas was still an 'infant' in law, subject to guardians, when plans were put forward to develop the Islington estate.

Much of Barnsbury's manorial land was copyhold, partly freed by an Act of 1822, under which tenants were enabled to 'improve' their land by building, or granting building leases, on payment of a third of a year's value of any houses they erected. In 1823 the guardians of young Thomas obtained licence to demise in order to build on their Islington fields.

From the south side of the Pied Bull, an ancient hostelry said to have been a country house of Sir Walter Raleigh's family, a footpath connected Upper Street with the Back Road at a point opposite where Cloudesley Square was very shortly laid out. Along this path (but starting north of the Pied Bull) the trustees proposed to lay a road, to be called Theberton Street, lined with 3rd-rate houses. From it would run two other small new roads of 4th-rate houses, Studd Street and Moon Street (1823–4).

These two humble service roads were the first to be built on the Milner-Gibson estate. Theberton Street south side followed in batches, mostly of six houses, between 1829 and 1836. The rest of the land was allotted to two squares, presumably as a means of accommodating the maximum number of houses on the awkwardly shaped fields. The estate surveyor and architect who laid out the site and designed the houses was Francis Edwards (1784–1857); but building was a protracted affair – perhaps because of a recession in the mid-1830s – and by the time the estate was finished in the 1840s two other architects had been employed (see *Milner Square*).

Edwards had been a pupil of Sir John Soane's, and also a student at the Royal Academy, where he won both a Silver and a Gold Medal (1808 and 1811), and continued to exhibit there for a number of years. At the time of the Milner-Gibson commission he was newly in his own practice, and had just designed gas-works at Hoxton for the Imperial Gas Company, and soon after, St John's Church at Hoxton.

Two interesting plans by Edwards of the estate exist, illustrating the odd shape of the land available for development. On the north-west, a triangle of land cut into it along the Back Road, tapering off to the north at the corner of Barnsbury Street. This belonged to George Pocock the dairy farmer, who had built there a row of small houses called Felix Place (1818), also Felix Terrace, a similar row on the opposite side of the road. On the north-east, five acres had been laid out in the late 18th century as a botanic garden by Dr William Pitcairn. The Milner-Gibson lands to be developed were thus very constricted and roughly T-shaped, extending in a broad band along the site of Theberton Street, with a narrower strip as the upright of the inverted T, running northwards at right angles to Barnsbury Street.

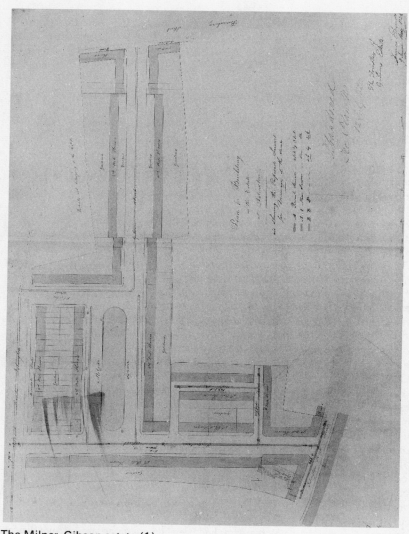

The Milner-Gibson estate (1)
Francis Edwards's proposed layout of 1824. Gibson Square appears as Milner
Square, Milner Square as Gibson Street

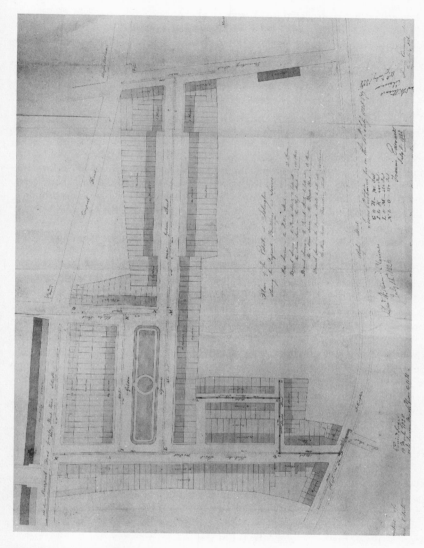

The Milner-Gibson estate (2)
The revised plan, 1828. House sites are all indicated, Gibson Square has its
present name, and Milner Square is still named Gibson Street

Edwards's first plan, dated 1824, shows Theberton, Studd and Moon Streets; Trinidad Place, a terrace along the Back Road estate boundary; and backing on to that, a long narrow rectangle which he called "Milner Square", its short south side forming part of Theberton Street. Linking the square's NW corner with the top end of Trinidad Place was Charles Street, and at the opposite corner a road continued northwards as "Gibson Street", broadening out into a second long 'square' – rather, two facing terraces – and then connecting by a short street with Barnsbury Street. Opposite Trinidad Place is "Cloudesley Terrace" (built 1819, now 83–199 Liverpool Road), the boundary of the adjoining Cloudesley estate.

The Barnsbury hilltop had once been dotted with pools, fed by local springs and used as 'ducking ponds', that is, for duck-hunting, although the laying out of house and street sewers in the current building boom was fast drying them up. A few still remained, however. Two were on the Milner-Gibson estate, although not shown on Edwards's plan: one in a field adjoining Felix Place, the other "a large deep pond" which survived until 1832, in a field some way up "whereon Charles Street Gibson Square now stands". These ponds are recorded by Tomlins, who lived at no. 3 Charles Street when it was first built, in a manuscript note in a copy of his *Perambulation of Islington* now at Islington Central Library.

The second and more elaborate plan by Edwards, dated 1 July, 1828, shows house and garden boundaries for the whole estate and renames the "Milner Square" of 1824 as Gibson Square. The Back Road has by now become Liverpool Road, and the Charles Street frontage has been slightly altered, but the second 'square' is still unnamed other than as set-back terraces of "Gibson Street".

Signed house plans now in the Middlesex Deeds Register suggest that Francis Edwards, besides laying out the estate, also designed the houses in Theberton Street south side and in Gibson Square. The street changes style slightly in places, reflecting its piecemeal creation, the earlier east and west ends (1829 and 1831) being of the favourite New River estate type with first-floor windows in circular-headed sunk panels. The distinctive Edwards style (see below) appears in the houses forming nos. 1–13 Gibson Square (renumbered in 1866 as 51–75 Theberton Street), built in 1831 as a free-standing terrace until the rest of the street caught up, though in keeping with the two long sides of the later square.

Gibson Square proper was completed in 1836–9, partly by Louis England, a local timber merchant, but the whole estate was finished only in the 1840s by Roumieu and Gough (see *Milner Square*). Since then it has suffered little serious change, and a few unworthy replacements have been rectified. One unmannerly rebuilding, with non-matching fenestration, was allowed in the 1960s of no. 18 Theberton Street at the corner of Moon Street. On the whole, however, the houses fortunately appear almost intact, many retaining such interior features as the original simple fireplaces, shutters, pine half-panelling, and folding doors between the downstairs parlours.

Later in the 19th century the solid middle-class occupants, tradesman-cum-professional, with a sprinkling of 'professors of music' and keepers of small private schools gave way to poorer ranks, and between the two world wars and for some time after the houses were tenemented by absentee landlords, often let in single rooms. Middle-class rediscovery and rehabilitation began in a small way in the 1950s and 1960s, until the whole area acquired a prosperous gloss such as it probably never enjoyed even in its pristine days.

In the early period of its renaissance the area was a favourite parking ground for lorry drivers on their way through London, many of whom stayed locally overnight, while the huge beached pantechnicons overshadowed two houses at a time even to their first-floor windows. This provoked an acrimonious residents' campaign, partly resolved when one of the chief drivers' lodgings, Bray's at 126/8 Liverpool Road, set up a lorry park near King's Cross, with a minibus service to the hostel. The problem had a tragic end when one night in November 1974 the building caught fire, thought to have been caused by a cigarette end, and 8 of the occupants died. The hostel was never reopened on the site, and the premises were not rebuilt until 1988 (see below).

Architecture

Gibson Square is distinctive even for Islington, notably in Francis Edwards's handsome pavilion blocks terminating the long sides. It is a long rectangle, of three storeys and basement except for the three central south side houses (61–65 Theberton Street) which have an extra storey. The south side consists of the 13 houses renumbered in 1866 as part of Theberton Street, and the north of an irregular terrace pushed off-centre. All houses have grooved stucco ground floors, bridged steps to the front doors, and balconies in a lacy anthemion design, mostly single, but double on the pavilion features. The square, built from west to east in 1836–9, has the coarser, heavier detail of a slightly later date, e.g. in window surrounds, than its earlier south side in Theberton Street. The latter (now 51–75) is still wholly in 1820s terrace style, distinguished only by its penultimate houses nos. 53 and 73, pilastered and pedimented – no. 53 has lost the pediment – a scaled-down version of the triple pavilions of the square proper. Nor have the central Theberton Street group, nos. 61–65, any distinguishing features other than their additional storey above a heavy cornice, with a low blocking course, and their being (like the terminal houses) slightly advanced, with the standard variation of circular-headed first-floor windows for rectangular.

It is the east and west sides that single out Gibson Square from other Islington squares – its terminating pavilion groups, almost flamboyantly Palladianesque as if incorporating some mansion, with cornice and pilasters, the central ones supporting a pediment, where the usual pair of windows is reduced to one, differently styled. On these sides too the centre blocks (nos. 23–26, 58–61) are distinguished only by circular-headed first-floor windows, and cornice, with mansard attics above. Centre

West side of Gibson Square, *c*. 1950
Francis Edwards's Palladianesque design for the 'pavilion' ends

and pavilion groups are, as usual, slightly advanced. Some houses retain a cast-iron hooped arch above their basement steps; the railings are mace-head and halberd.

At the NE corner, nos. 44–49 continue beyond the square to link with Milner Place in a minor key, by two houses with a cornice. The west side shows signs of settlement in a couple of places (nos. 18, 25).

The north side, at first sight less original, is really a kind of architectural joke: it is not centred on the square, but shunted to the west by the Milner Place exit, and exhibits a kind of dogged determination somehow to fit in a complete terrace at all costs. All features are there, the rhythm 2-4-2-4-2, the slightly advanced end houses with blocking courses, with the usual circular-headed drawing-room windows (here minus the heavy surrounds of the E and W sides). At the NE corner nos. 42/43 have lost their cornice and original upper-floor windows, no. 42 having a clumsy insert; nos. 36/37 and 35E-F uniquely have gothic upper panes instead of the usual radial. High chimney stacks above the central houses suggest that they, too, were intended to have attics, never built.

The western exit was originally named Charles Street (on the site of Tomlins's recorded 'ducking pond' which was presumably drained and levelled off); from 1873 it was incorporated into Gibson Square numbering, but as there were no numbers left it was numbered 35A, B, C and D. Further, when the corner house of Liverpool Road, burnt out in 1974 was finally rebuilt in 1988, two replica houses were added on its back yard space by James Gorst, as a further terminating pair to the terrace, with blocking course, stuccoing, balconettes, astragals and all, and though adjoining no. 35A, had to be numbered 35E and F. Beyond again, the double block, also by James Gorst, now infilling 126b Liverpool Road on the site of the former Bray's transport hostel, with a touch of the Egyptian and Art Deco but blending happily with the surroundings, bears the date-plaque "Gibson Square 1988".

At the square's NE exit, presumably left unfinished by Edwards, the influence of Roumieu and Gough begins to make itself felt: Milner Place is already noticeably Milnerish, while the end door of no. 35 Gibson Square, like no. 43, is distinctively rectangular in Roumieu and Gough style.

The Gardens and 'Temple'

Francis Edwards's plan for Gibson Square shows a boringly conventional layout for the central garden, surrounded like other London squares by railings with locked gates, open only to resident key-holders. In the 1930s, when the square was run-down and impoverished, the residents handed over the gardens to Islington Council for upkeep, and during the war it was dug up for air-raid shelters. Afterwards it was restored, replanted and well maintained, if again conventional in design.

The simulated temple now in the gardens, with Pantheon overtones, is a ventilating shaft for the Victoria Line of London Underground. It is also a milestone in the battle for the environment, marking an early conservation victory for the district.

In 1963, when London Transport was about to build the new line, sites were earmarked for ventilation shafts in open spaces, including Fitzroy and Gibson Squares. The former was in private hands, and compensation was offered. Gibson Square, safely (it was supposed) owned by the Council, was presented with an arbitrary proposal for a 50-foot ventilating tower of grimly functional design and clad in exposed aggregate concrete panels. London Transport engineers, expecting to deal with uninterested landlords of run-down tenancies, were to their surprise confronted by a well-organised gang of angry and articulate new owner-occupiers, who formed a society, fought an apparently doomed campaign for several years, and carried the fight to the office of the Minister of Transport in person with the support of, among others, Sir Basil Spence.

London Transport progressively modified the design and lowered the height, both pronounced impossible in the first instance. The eventual low-rise structure, completed in 1970, was designed by Raymond Erith with Quinlan Terry, then a junior partner, as a pedimented temple front with niches and dome-like mesh roof. Its brick has mellowed over the years to a well-nigh authentic Georgian pastiche, generally admired. The gardens, occupied by the building works for several years, were restored by London Transport to their pre-vent shaft form, with the additional

Gibson Square, north side in 1965
showing high chimney stacks where a further storey was originally intended.
In 1988 the terrace was extended to link with Liverpool Road

replacement of bona fide railings for the post-war chicken-wire netting; and repaving with York stone slabs.

Excavation for the ventilation shaft had meanwhile caused great disruption for more than a year; the new railway line cut diagonally below the houses from NE to SW, and has caused some settlement.

Inhabitants

Gibson Square early proved more notable for its architecture than its residents, with a history of modest obscurity, peopled by families who would fit well as minor Dickensian or Thackerayan characters. One of some fame in early Victorian times was Samuel Maunder (1785–1849), compiler of music, who lived at no. 67 from 1843 until his death.

Thomas Milner-Gibson (1806–84), although never a resident, merits a few words on his career. He was MP from 1837 to 1868 (with one short interval) successively for Ipswich, Manchester, and Ashton-under-Lyne, and was an active anti-Corn Laws campaigner; from 1859–66 he was President of the Board of Trade. He was a friend of Charles Dickens and Benjamin Disraeli, and was also a keen sailor, in his yacht the *Resolute*. A tablet in the English church at Algiers commemorates the fact that he was the last to sail in the Mediterranean with a permit from the Bey of Algiers. He died on board his own yacht.

Thomas Edlyn Tomlins, author of *A Perambulation Through Islington* (1858), was living in that year and until 1875 at 3 Charles Street, Gibson Square.

In more modern times the distinguished photographer Angus McBean bought no. 34 in 1945, and later also the adjoining no. 35, living there for some years before taking a studio in Colebrooke Row and moving to Suffolk. He was one of the pioneers of Barnsbury's revival as a popular residential suburb.

Highbury Crescent (1844–50)

In March 1840 the protective covenants and sub-leases granted by John Dawes to John Spiller on the building of Highbury Place expired. With the removal of restriction, building development now became possible on the space opposite to it, backing on to Holloway Road. In 1844 James Wagstaffe, the Canonbury builder and surveyor, secured 99-year building leases from the then freeholder, Dawes's descendant Henry Dawes, for a plot bordering Highbury fields on the west, while still not encroaching on the amenities of Highbury Place. He drew up a plan for substantial villas in large gardens along a crescent – its shape dictated by the site – and supervised their design and building.

James Goodbody, a solicitor, took over the houses in blocks, probably in carcase, and sub-leased. The 25 houses, mostly paired, were built by local or imported builders, starting at either end of the new road, the middle houses last: the first ones let to Goodbody (January 1846) were the top seven, nos. 19–25; by 1847 10 houses were occupied, by 1848 18, and the last seven were finished in 1849 and 1850. No. 1, Highbury Lodge, was excepted from the letting agreement with Goodbody and was let direct to Wagstaffe for his own occupation.

At the same time Wagstaffe was introducing the semi-detached elsewhere in Islington, with Belitha Villas, considerably less ambitious, in Barnsbury; soon afterwards he concluded agreements in Canonbury for building the 'Alwyne' group of roads, also in modest villa style. Highbury Crescent, however, semi-detached or no, is undoubtedly grand. It consists of pairs of houses in large blocks with a variety of decorative features, largely Italianate: seen from up the hill they are almost like a row of vast liners anchored side by side.

Some have been destroyed. No. 25 was replaced in 1937 by Crescent Mansions, a block of flats; nos. 21/22 are now a derelict gap site, and nos. 4 and 5/6 have given way to Council office blocks, 5/6 now named Highbury House, the Social Services Department. Unfortunately the two free-standing villas, Wagstaffe's house and no. 2, disappeared under extensions to Highbury Station (the original Great Northern and City (Electric) Railway was built in 1906). No. 4 vanished with the rear enlargement of the Highbury Imperial Picture Theatre, first built in 1912 at 2 Holloway Road. From 1902–74 no. 3 was the home of a Sandemanian or Glasite meeting house. Several of the properties have had later houses and flats built in their once extensive back gardens.

Architecture

Of the survivors, the top pair (23/24) have circular-headed windows, and Tuscan porches with triglyph frieze and dentil moulding. The ground floor has large four-light windows, and the central feature on each floor is a rusticated blind niche, on the ground floor a panel rather than niche. Nos. 19/20 are similar but slightly smaller, their windows of standard rectangular bracketed style. No. 20 retains its rusticated porch with keystone arch, no. 19's has been replaced with a more modern one.

The two pairs 15/16 and 17/18, flanking Fieldway Crescent, are the grandest and most assertive, each bounded by a pair of low 'towers' bordered with coigns, providing an additional low storey with pyramidal roof. The front doors with Doric porticoes are in a further small wing (mostly altered and added to). Ground floors have angular bays, and paired circular-headed windows above with brackets and rosettes, but No. 17's fenestration has been altered throughout, with an extra bay and additional windows. Nos. 15 and 16 retain a few unusual astragals with margin panes.

The less interesting nos. 13/14 have shallow bays and crowded fenestration, and broad cill bands at all levels. No. 13 has also acquired a large lower addition with rusticated stucco ground floor.

Highbury Crescent in 1844
Shown shortly after its building, in handsome groups of paired Italianate villas.
The architect was James Wagstaffe

Nos. 11/12, more elegant, have stuccoed ground floor, flattened bows with balustrated tops, and shallowly pedimented windows above; most of the other upper windows are round-headed Italianate, in twos and threes. Front doors with Doric porches are in an extension (12 has a balustrade above).

Nos. 7/8, 9/10 are also two pairs, plainish but handsome, with an advanced centre, stuccoed ground floor and Doric porches similar to no. 11's. One first-floor window in each has a high, almost conical pediment; the ground-floor windows have lying panes. An extension has been added to no. 10 – early this century?

The bottom end of the Crescent is generally tackier. Two unattractive office blocks fill the place of the next three houses, and no. 3, long in the possession of J. Murphy & Sons, builders and engineers, is in a run-down state, though in the summer of 1992 an application was made for its conversion into offices, and in August restoration work began. It is the one remaining single villa, in style more traditional than the rest of the flamboyantly fashionable crescent, handsomely plain with rusticated coigns and bracketed windows, and a lower extension to the south (a presumably matching wing to the north has been replaced by a modern addition). During its period as a chapel a large meetings room was created by throwing the whole top floor into one, and raising the existing ceiling to replace it with another of fine vaulted timber.

Highbury Park Terrace, 23–61 Highbury Park (1829; 1831–6)

In the 1820s Highbury House and its lands were acquired from Mr John Bentley by Robert Felton, a City seed merchant, of Lawrence Pountney Lane, who then became bankrupt, and from 1826 gradually sold off the fringes of the estate. Certain tracts passed via assignees to different purchasers, but the portion on which Park Terrace was built has not so far been traced; nor, surprisingly in view of its dignified appearance, has the architect or even builder been identified.

The site was a strip of land set back from the hilltop road beyond Highbury Barn, and it was designed as a long terrace of 20 houses in heavily classical style. It appears on Cruchley's map of 1829, though Cromwell remarks in 1835 that "several are as yet unfinished" (p. 308). They were complete by Lewis's time (1842). The Rate Books show fairly gradual progress, nos. 3 and 5 appearing in 1829, empty, and no others being recorded until 1831/2. 1832 shows nos. 1–6 as complete and the rest seem to follow by 1835 and 1836.

The roadway has remained unmade, above street level with a retaining wall and a strip of grass and a row of chestnut trees. The name alternated as Park Terrace and Highbury Park, confirmed as the latter (nos. 23–61) in 1877, after a complaint by the Metropolitan Board of Works that no less than seven streets were named "Highbury Park".

Highbury Park Terrace
A main-road terrace with interesting features, begun in 1829
From a postcard view of *c.* 1910

The terrace is among the most elaborate in Islington, and by far the most Grecian. Houses are four floors and basement, ground floor in channelled stucco with cill band above; ground floor windows and front doors are segmental – though, oddly, no. 45 is square-headed. Other windows are rectangular. The wide doors have Tuscan columns and frieze, with fanlights compressed into narrow segments. Below the top floor runs a continuous cornice. The end bays of the end houses, 23 and 61, containing the front doors, are set back, no. 23 with a columned portico, 61 with a square pilastered porch.

Close study reveals a remarkable variety of plan and detail, probably due to the staggered building dates. No. 23, the first house, is 3-bay, next come 10 2-bay (25–41), and the next two pairs, whose doorways are set together (43/45, 47/49) all 3-bay; furthermore no. 41 and the larger 47/49 have an elaborate honeysuckle frieze under the cornice, now lost from the intervening houses, and the five houses 41–49 are all very slightly set forward like a centrepiece, while 41–45 have more elaborate rustication than the rest – yet 41 is an odd-man-out with only two bays. Confusing, to put it mildly. From 51 to the end are all 3-bay except no. 55 which is four, and is further enriched by a portico repeating the door design, and marble steps.

A few mouldings have been lost, such as the cornice on no. 53, and at nos. 55 and 61 the top windows have been lengthened, cutting into the cornice moulding below.

101

The whole terrace shows signs of being knocked about over the years. Nos. 39–45 possibly never had balconies, but the last three have acquired sets of four plain railings, as simple as those in New Terrace (Duncan Terrace). The rest of the terrace has single splayed balconies with long palmettes in a mesh surround.

Highbury Place (1774–7)

Highbury Place was initiated by the Canonbury stockbroker, John Dawes, who owned the pastoral land in Highbury fields beyond Islington village's northern boundary of Hopping Lane. Dawes built Highbury House for himself in 1778–81, and lived there until his death in 1788 (demolished 1938: Eton House, Leigh Road is now on the site). Meanwhile, in 1774 or perhaps earlier, Dawes leased ground to John Spiller, who started building a row of sophisticated houses to run up the shallow slope of the fields, intending a terrace with a frontage of 978 feet.

When the first six houses were completed, Spiller used them as security to borrow money from Dawes to continue. The assignments of 67-year leases were made chiefly to Robert Mackreth, a Hampshire gentleman, and John Spiller, builder in Islington, formerly of Christ Church parish, Southwark. By July 1774 two terraces, flanking six linked villas, were built: two more, that is, than the original intention. The top house, no. 24, had an 81-foot frontage, part of which was used for a coach-house and outbuildings (see below, p. 109). A further terrace, to no. 39, was completed by 1777 and let to Spiller under 15 separate leases. No. 39, the top house of all, Spiller had for himself.

The amenities of this urban excursion into the country were carefully guarded: in 1778 Dawes guaranteed to Spiller and his sub-lessees that for the entire period of the leases, the land opposite the new houses should remain open as far as the road to Holloway and be used for nothing more permanent than the brick-works set up for building the row. Later, a set of gates and a lodge for this private street guarded the entrance from the main Islington road.

The houses were probably designed by John Spiller's son James (d. 1829), a pupil of James Wyatt and later associated with Soane. At this time James Spiller was near the start of his career; his later works included additional buildings for the London Hospital in Whitechapel Road (1781–3), St John's Church, Hackney (1792–7), and revised designs for the London Institution in Albemarle Street (1800–1801). Some of Spiller's work, notably Hackney Church, showed great originality, but he appears to have been such a prickly perfectionist that his output was not great. His brothers Robert and John, who were masons and sculptors, may also have been engaged in the building at Highbury. John junior at least lived in Highbury Place at one time.

For years the long terraces stood in the fields in solitary splendour, an elegant row combining urbane regularity with considerable variety. The topmost range, indeed,

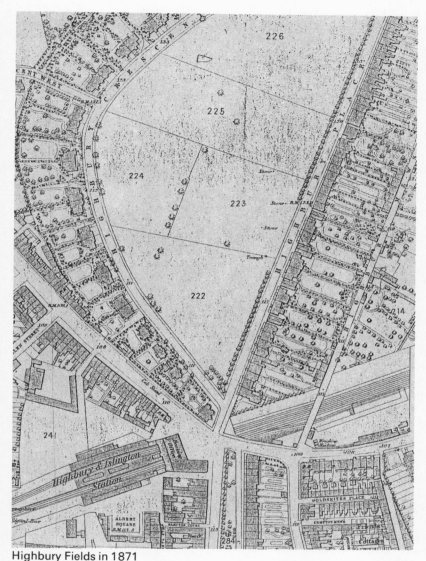

Highbury Fields in 1871
The first Ordnance Survey shows the area still uninterrupted by the building of
Calabria Road, and the end villas of Highbury Crescent undisturbed by the
Underground Station. Albert Square is just south of the railway station, and
Compton Square, bottom right corner, east of Compton Terrace

might fit comfortably into the precincts of some prosperous country town. When in 1789 a new terrace was built on the other side of the fields, the protective clause in the contract ensured that Highbury Terrace extended from a point just north of Highbury Place.

This was the limit of 18th-century building investment here, and whereas in Canonbury Dawes's building indirectly encouraged the inception of a square, the terraces on Highbury fields were still isolated rows in the 1820s when Thomas Cubitt made his first building foray farther east. Even when the 67-year leases fell in, the only houses built within view of Highbury Place were to be the grand set of villas forming Highbury Crescent (1840s). Still more fortunately, the fields largely survived the building rash of the 1860s and later, until the remnant of $27\frac{1}{2}$ acres was saved as a public park in 1885 and 1891. We thus have the possibly unique experience of seeing two 18th-century terraces in a time capsule, undeveloped and, apart from the major disturbance round the centre of the Place, little changed.

The building history of Highbury Place was uneventful until the 1870s, when the Great Northern Railway obtained permission to run a tunnel diagonally under the fields (in the stretch between Drayton Park and Canonbury Stations), demolishing one of Spiller's pairs of villas to accommodate it and altering much of the back premises (1873). In the next decade further destruction was allowed with the building of Calabria Road, approved in 1887, as part of a small estate laid out by a builder, H. Baylis. Its Roman colonial street-names were oddly chosen by the Trustees of the Metropolitan Board of Works — Liberia, Baalbec, Calabria — perhaps commemorating the fictitious Roman camp popularly supposed to have existed at Highbury. Baalbec Road led into the Fields slightly north of Highbury Place, but its parallel, Calabria Road, cut right through it, tacking itself on to the corner and wrecking the symmetry.

A lesser though still unfortunate spoliation occurred in 1888 when another builder, J. C. Hill of 22 Archway Road, secured permission to convert the top pair of villas (now 13/15) into shops, which from 1890 appear in the Directories. A still further intrusion was the introduction of shop fronts into the adjoining terrace by Morton Bros, piano dealers, from 1901 at no. 19, extending in 1923 to nos. 18–20 with huge, incongruous plate glass windows removed only in the 1980s.

Early sale advertisements for reversions of leases describe the scope and use of rooms and gardens. No. 13, advertised for auction in *The Oracle* on 3 July 1792, with 48 years unexpired, ground rent 8 guineas, is described as "containing eight good Bed-Chambers, and Closets, a light Drawing-room; elegant Dining-room, 21 feet by 17; Dining Parlour, Breakfast Room, neat Entrance Hall, Kitchen, wash-house, Laundry, Pantry, Dairy, Footman's Room, and good Cellars". It also had "a five Stall-Stable, Coach-House, Yard", and large walled garden "well stocked with standard and Wall Fruit Trees".

In October 1808 the slightly less grand no. 36 was advertised as with a handsome dining-room, good drawing-room, breakfast parlour, and six bedrooms; store-room,

Highbury Place in 1835
The entrance from Highbury Corner
from the engraving by J. & H. S. Storer

kitchen and scullery, wash-house, and wine, coal and beer cellars and two-stall stable. The earlier reference to a footman's room is an interesting indication of the fashionable standing of this pioneer of "first-rate" town houses, not even in a suburb but in the country.

*　　*　　*

The original pattern of the Place was:
1774 period: 1–9 (terrace), 10/11, 12/13, 14/15 (paired villas), 16–24 (terrace);
1777 period: 25–39 (terrace).
Calabria Road destroyed the original nos. 12/13, and the present nos. 12–15 have endured the complex modifications described below.

Architecture
As Highbury Place was built in two nearly continuous stages, there are expected differences between the second (nos. 25–39) and first (nos. 1–24) stages. Even the first, however, is in two distinct parts. First, the similarities.

The houses are 3-storey and basement, many also having attics under mansard roofs, and mostly 3-bay, in unstuccoed stock brick, with little stone dressing. The exceptions to three bays are the paired villas and the ends of terraces, each 5-bay (except in the top terrace nos. 25–39).

Apart from the door-surrounds, features are square-headed, and the front doors are wide, with impost blocks and keystones, approached by railed flights of steps. None have balconies. Many houses have lost their astragals, but a number still have original shutters and some, wrought-iron lamp-holders.

Many houses also have back extensions, probably contemporary or at least early 19th century, and much simple interior panelling survives, without decoration and very practical, with numerous wall-cupboards. Ceiling mouldings and friezes are similarly unpretentious.

End houses have front-door extensions, usually altered (nos. 1, 9, 10, 23; no. 15 is swallowed up by the Evangelical Church (see below, (e). The low, pedimented coach-houses originally separating the terraces remain in varying states. Those between nos. 9 and 10 are perfectly recognisable, and even better preserved are the pair between nos. 24 and 25, which was allotted extra space (see above, p. 102). At nos. 15A, 16A, later infilling has obscured the originals.

I   *The original Place (nos. 1–24)* was designed almost symmetrically as a balancing terrace on either side of three pairs of large linked villas, and with coach-houses between. (The slightly later top terrace, nos. 25–39, somewhat blurs this pattern.) To-day that layout is hard to interpret, largely due to the intrusion of Calabria Road, but also because of the house divisions, window alterations and complex renumbering in the central part, and butchery of the top pair of villas (now the various nos. 13–15).

(a) Starting at Highbury Corner, the *lowest terrace (nos. 1–9)* is of 3-bay houses, bounded at either end by a large 5-bay house (nos. 1, 9) with single-storey front-door extension. No. 1 from 1927–31 was the artist Sickert's, adapted as his studio, with not only a massive Ionic porch but a two-bay single-storey extension beyond. The ground floors of nos. 2–4 have been altered, no. 2 with an ebullient shop front, no. 3 with a very ordinary one (though retaining its original front door), no. 4 with an aggressive Victorian frontage in red brick with yellow stone dressings, keystones and pilasters, completely cutting away the cill-band.

(b) Between no. 9 and the first pair of monumental villas are the first two *coach-houses* (appropriately numbered 9 and 10 Coach House), retaining their single-storey pedimented form above large circular-headed entrances, later converted into workshops; now windows.

(c) *Nos. 10 and 11* are the *first linked villas*, five-bay, plain with a cill-band below the first floor. Each pair was long enough to rank almost as a short terrace. This first pair survives pretty well and shows how the central group of houses would

Highbury Place

Highbury Place
Some of the large paired villas designed by James Spiller for John Dawes. The low gabled building was originally stables. Beyond is the corner of Calabria Road (1887), for which two villas were demolished. Postcard view, *c.* 1910

have looked originally. No. 10 has acquired a florid Italianate porch (*c.* 1860) with square Ionic pilasters, while retaining its ground-floor shutters; no. 11 has a smallish doorway with bracketed lintel.

(d) Here starts the complication. Loss of the *two central villas* to railway development, and tampering with the top pair, have been the worst violations to Highbury Place. The successor to the central pair is simply an open space hidden behind hoardings with a single small free-standing gabled building (no. 11A), workshop style, possibly about 1890.

(e) Beyond this is Calabria Road, no. 1 of whose 1890 houses is attached to no. 13 Highbury Place; and the *top pair of Spiller's villas* (now nos. 13/14 and 14A/15 + 15B & C) are so embedded and meddled with that they take some deciphering.

Both these 5-bay houses have been divided into two of two bays, and their ground floors stuccoed; 13/14 each with a pair of clumsy pastiche 'Georgian' windows too closely set (query, why could they not have matched the originals?). Small front doors with rectangular 3-circle fanlights have been inserted – a style quite foreign to Highbury Place – and Victorian bathroom windows above.

The 14/15 complex has remains of the old 1890 shop fronts made when Calabria Road was built: no. 14A an ugly five-light window, no. 15 retaining shop-front fascia and brackets above, with a new small 'Georgian' door (15B, C) on one side and a grandiose new doorcase on the other, which balances that of the Evangelical Church (see below). Above, on each floor the central window of the original five has been blocked up.

(f) Finally, nos. 15A and 16A are an infilling of *coach-house* spaces, 15A a narrow 1870s house carried to the height of the terrace, with an ornamental-headed triple window above and stuccoed ground floor. No. 16A, the Evangelical Brotherhood Church, must incorporate the original ground floor but was given a grand entrance and raised by one storey in the 19th century.

(g) *Nos. 16–24.* This terrace is now unfortunately joined to the next buildings below, but balances nos. 1–9, with front door positions reversed: features are broad cill-bands, and circular doorcases with impost blocks carrying a keystone arch. Several houses (16, 21–23) retain their arched cast-iron lampholders. No. 24, originally the 5-bay closing feature, has been sub-divided and now looks 3-bay, and in the mid-1950s its front-door extension was given a pastiche Tuscan porch in fibre-glass; a bayed room has been built above. The chief violation in this terrace for many years was the incongruous plate-glass shop windows of nos. 18–20; even when the houses became the architects' offices Eastwyke Field they remained unchanged. They have now been restored and converted into offices, the use of old bricks to replace the original style of the ground-floor fronts achieving a well-nigh invisible patching.

The last *coach-house block* is attached to nos. 24 and 25, otherwise with no numbering. It is wider and less altered than the others, still with its plain low double doors instead of a later front-door-style insertion at the sides like nos. 9 and 10.

II   *Nos. 25–39.* This terrace, later and longer than the rest, has suffered least change, even retaining most of its astragals (except 27, 29, 34). Again the end houses, nos. 25 and 39 (here only 3-bay) balance one another, and have three widely spaced windows and horizontal cill-bands, but they are not a pair: no. 25 (Joseph Chamberlain's house) has ground-floor windows recessed in semi-circular arches in a style similar to that much used on the New River estate and elsewhere some half-century later. No. 39, Spiller's own house, has a pilastered central front door, villa-style, and is crowned by a cornice and blocking course, until recently terminated with urns. It may originally have had the usual front-door extension, but an elaborate stuccoed façade in neo-Greek style was added in the early 19th century as a grand frontispiece and vista-closer to the road across the fields, with open pediment, frieze, dentil cornice and acroteria. In 1979 another house was built behind this frontispiece, slightly set back (no. 40), then a second; finally comes a red-brick Gothic Baptist chapel (1887), with lancets and steep gable, removed here from Providence Chapel, Islington Green.

In the main part of the terrace the central house, no. 32, has an elaborate Tuscan portico with rusticated door-surround, rather over-icing the cake. Most of the front doors are crowned with skeletal pediments or gables within stucco surrounds, a few (27, 30, 31, 34 and 35) variously elaborated. Nos. 38 and 39 have iron lamp-holders; no. 28 has been refitted with later Gothick panes, and its drawing-room floor windows lengthened.

Inhabitants
From its earliest days Highbury Place was an exclusive residential quarter, with a good share of distinguished residents.

At *no. 1* from 1927–31 the painter Walter Sickert, RA (1860–1942) kept a studio and a school of painting.

At *no. 25* from 1845–54 lived the Rt Hon. Joseph Chamberlain (1836–1914), one-time Colonial Secretary and father of Sir Austen and Neville Chamberlain. In the 1770s, when the house belonged to John Horton, John Wesley used to stay there.

No. 14 was the house for almost the last half-century of his life of John Nichols (1744–1826), author of *Literary Anecdotes of the 18th Century* and of a history of Canonbury (1788), and long co-editor with Edward Cave of *The Gentleman's Magazine*.

No. 28 was the house of Samuel Lewis, Junior, author of *The History . . . of the Parish of St Mary Islington* (1842) and other Islington works.

At *no. 32* from 1850–81 lived the Egyptologist Samuel Sharpe (1790–1881), who also made a translation of the Bible.

No. 38 belonged to Abraham Newland (1730–1807), Chief Cashier of the Bank of England from 1782; and like Spiller a native of Southwark. Newland kept this house as a country retreat, living over the Bank and driving up here, it was said, daily to drink tea with his housekeeper and returning to the City to sleep. Another banker, William Ward (1787–1843), born in Highbury Place, became a Director of the Bank of England and a foreign exchange expert.

The top house, *no. 39*, was occupied by the builder of Highbury Place, John Spiller.

Another inhabitant was Thomas Wilson (1746–1843), treasurer of Highbury Baptist College, who financed the building of several chapels including Claremont Chapel, Pentonville Road (1819), and died at *no. 12*. His son Joshua lived at *no. 35*.

From 1880–1900 the pastor of Providence Chapel was the Revd Philip Reynolds, whose daughter Bessie in 1889 published a novel, *Loaves and Fishes*, reflecting the chapel and its congregation too closely for comfort – so that her father found it necessary to resign. A number of his congregation, however, left with him.

The Fields

Contemporary views show the tranquil origins of the area, now the only sizeable piece of open ground to survive in Islington. Rustic haymakers and sheep appear as the only occupants, though as the fields lay alongside the main road from the North, it was a regular stopping place for cattle to graze on the way to or from Smithfield, a couple of miles away. In the 19th century the ground was pressed into service as allotments for inhabitants, in place of kitchen gardens, though by Islington standards the back gardens were generous. For many years an arched conduit head covered a spring in front of no. 14, the house of John Nichols, its waters like that of many local springs channelled to serve the City.

In 1885, $25\frac{1}{4}$ acres of the remaining open land were purchased from John Dawes's descendants by Islington Vestry and opened to the public, after the failure of a long campaign to acquire a much larger area north of London, which would have secured a magnificent tract of parkland in perpetuity as "Albert Park". The welcome if pathetic remnant of Highbury Fields is the sole survivor of this unsuccessful attempt. A further two and a half acres were acquired in 1891 on the demolition of Highbury Grove, a mansion next to Terrace Field at the northern end. In the succeeding century these $27\frac{3}{4}$ acres have remained Islington's largest open space, and heavily used in consequence, for circuses, Bonfire Night fireworks, air raid shelters, rock concerts and carnivals.

In 1921 an open-air swimming-pool was opened near the south end of the Fields, followed by tennis courts. The pool was closed for modernisation in 1981, but because of technical difficulties was finally reopened, as an indoor pool, only in 1984. Creation of recreational facilities, and the felling of diseased elm-trees in 1975 and later (with replanting), provoked successive outcries at 'erosion' of the precious space, and a Residents' Association was formed in the 1970s, local opinion usually being divided between seeing such developments as 'improvement' or threat.

In 1905 a memorial was erected at the south entrance to the Fields, to Islington men who fell in the South African War, in the form of a bronze figure of Victory holding a wreath. The sculptor was Bertram McKennal, RA, and the model for the figure was his wife.

The Fields, which have never been landscaped as a park, remain one of several small remnants of the open tracts which used to surround London and are now a characteristic of neighbouring suburbs such as Hoxton and Hackney. They lend a character and charm to the dignified terraces on the perimeter, ringed with mature trees, like a faded glimpse of the rural suburb of two centuries ago.

Highbury Terrace (1789–94 and 1817)

This is a pioneer in the genre of Islington terraces. It deploys a sophisticated, urban building style in the country, almost contemporary with the (now almost vanished) suburb of Pentonville. When built, it was well beyond Islington, then a straggling main-road village clustered around church and green on the threshold of the Great North Road. John Dawes, who some 14 years earlier had built the stylish Highbury Place combining terraces with linked villas, here launched into a continuous high-rise, Bath-type terrace of four storeys and basement. But though the finishings were elegant, the material was London brick, rather jerry-built at that. It was intended for well-to-do merchants, bankers and professional men who fancied a country back-ground rather than home-life over their City offices, hence it was designed as an entity: centre group with low linking blocks to the 'wings' – echoes, too, of the grander Paragon in Blackheath.

The terrace was the first addition to Highbury fields after completion of Highbury Place, and because of Dawes's covenant with Spiller, starts at a point north of it, so that they are not facing. It was only begun in the year after John Dawes's death, but although it was built over a period and by two or three builders its effect is harmonious and integrated. First completed were nos. 1–16 (1789–94); nos. 17–20 show differences of detail, and the much later nos. 21 and 22, built in 1817, have distinct modifications.

Architecture

In contrast with Highbury Place the Terrace is tall and narrow, yet the houses are three-bay, their windows uneasily crowded and the effect is more urban. The houses are of stock brick with stone dressings. The layout is of two similar blocks, nos. 3–13 and 17–22, linked by a central block of three (nos. 14–16) with a tablet bearing the name and year in huge incised lettering. In this central group the ground-floor

Highbury Terrace
Begun in 1789 for John Dawes, its north range not completed until 1817.
Between about 1801 and 1834 the terrace had an early residents' association
From a contemporary engraving

windows are circular-headed, and first-floor windows shorter than the rest. In the other houses, first-floor windows are exceptionally tall (like the NW side of Canonbury Square), and as in Highbury Place, all square-headed, except in nos. 1 and 2 and in the south end block. Fanlights are standard of 'cobweb' style. Unlike the Place, however, windows in the S block have window-guards (except no. 13), in simple bowed shape of upright bars bounded by rows of circles.

Nos. 1 and 2, considerably more elaborate than the rest, are really paired villas, the entrances in side wings to which upper storeys have been added, presumably later, each with three windows. The round-headed ground-floor windows are in arched recesses with string-courses, a first-floor cill band, and cornice above the second floor. The keystones of the arched front doors are Coade-stone masks, and no. 1 also has Coade-stone impost blocks. The garden front has bow windows, a rare feature in Islington houses.

The first block (3–13) continues the cornice and parapet but has squared windows and doors, first-floor windows in arched recesses, and the doorways also arched in recesses — except no. 8, with dressed stucco ground floor and door surround; the surrounds stuccoed except for no. 12, which has a timber Ionic portico carrying a flat roof with wrought iron frieze. No. 11 has a 'Barnsbury'-type 'teardrop' fanlight. Some windows, notably nos. 11–13, have lost their astragals.

Separating nos. 16 and 17 is a low screen of three arches, one a garden entrance, the centre one blank, flanked by circular-headed niches, and the third altered — presumably once an entrance to no. 17.

The northern block (17–22) is irregular, no. 17 being a double house of six bays, with wide doorways and elaborate fanlights, its cill-band higher and first-floor windows quite short. In the later nos. 21 and 22 (evidently by a different builder) the windows are slightly higher, with a diglyph frieze and brick cornice, the upper floors oddly blank, with only two windows each. Nos. 17–18, which between them have 10 windows across, have window-guards of plain lattice shape. Nos. 18–20 are four-bay; no. 18 has a Doric timber portico. The end wall (no. 22) is filled with blind segmental windows, the lowest three enclosed in arches.

Inhabitants
Early residents include Charles Apthorp Wheelwright, last Commander of the Loyal Islington Volunteers, formed like many similar associations as a civilian corps against Napoleon.

At no. 1, from 1796 until his death in 1806, lived Francis Ronalds, a merchant, father of the pioneer of the electric telegraph. The latter, who became Sir Francis (1788–1873), is said to have experimented with a cable linking the rear coach-house with a nearby cottage.

At no. 12 lived Captain Joseph Huddart from 1792 until his death in 1816, geographer and hydrographer, who charted many oceans; one of the elder brethren of Trinity House, a planner of the East India Docks, and in earlier life an employee of the East India Company. He had a small observatory with a telescope in his attic from which height he could view the Thames and new Docks.

Colonel Edward Wigan, who lived at no. 19 until his death in 1814, was Common Councillor for the Ward of Cheap, and a Lt Colonel in the West London Militia. After his death his widow and then his daughter continued to live in the house, while his son, also Edward, lived at no. 9.

Later, no. 18 from 1916 to 1938 was the Elizabeth Fry Home for Girls; while nos. 1 and 2 served as a "Home for Confirmed Invalids" (the Highbury Home), formerly at other addresses, from 1900 to 1975. (In 1900 it was no. 1 only, from 1901 nos. 1 and 2, and for a time from 1907 also at no. 3) From 1907–15 a Salvation Army Rescue Home occupied no. 17.

An early Residents' Association

An interesting documentary survival is one of the Minute Books, 1812–34, of a Highbury Terrace Residents' Association, founded in 1801 or possibly earlier. Their preoccupations are both illuminating and curiously familiar. An annually elected Treasurer held meetings at his own house during his term of office and administered the subscription fund, while residents paid according to the size of their house, the larger nos. 1, 2 and 14–22 paying more than the rest. At first the subscription tended to rise, perhaps with the wartime cost of living, though the 4 and $4\frac{1}{2}$ guineas of 1813 was for an exceptional expense; 3 and $3\frac{1}{2}$ guineas was more normal.

Besides a lamp-lighter and street sweeper, who also looked after the mews, the Terrace employed two and later three watchmen, and for a time a superintendent, armed with rattles, muskets and cutlasses. Two of these were to keep watch during the night (usually 10 p.m.–6 a.m. in winter, 5 a.m. in summer). There was also a 'Patrol' (one man) who came on duty from sunset until the watch was set. The watchmen were expected to call the hour when coming on and going off duty, and supposedly at quarter-hour intervals. Their pay was usually about 14/– a week, 16/– in winter, and new greatcoats were provided every three years. The duties were frequently reviewed, notably when a couple of houses were burgled in 1813, in 1823, and more spectacularly in 1828, when some plate was stolen. On that occasion the watchmen were not thought to be implicated, but were dismissed as "highly negligent and culpable", one being drunk and all three asleep.

An Act for watching and lighting the parish had been passed in 1806, and most established streets were adopted by the parish and rated for these services. It is a sign either of the Terrace's isolation, or its deliberate independence, that its residents undertook these responsibilities for so long. Besides keeping the street and mews swept and clear of rubbish, they had to provide the lighting, and from time to time paid for a new lamp-post or had the watch-boxes at either end painted and repaired. They also contributed a sum to Highbury Place residents for road repairs.

Only in 1818 did the Terrace consider applying for adoption to the commissioners, who had meanwhile left them alone. It now appeared that the Act covered only those parts of Islington not yet watched and lighted, and as the Terrace had for so long provided these services they considered themselves exempt, particularly as in the 12 years since the Act no assessment had been made. There was a burst of activity while the residents conferred with Highbury Place, consulted a lawyer, and approached their landlord Mr Henry Dawes, for financial backing for a private Act of Parliament, to keep them exempt from the parish expenses and regulations. The gesture fizzled out when Dawes declared (May 1820) that he would not after all add more than £100 to the £200 they had themselves raised, so the idea of a private Bill was dropped.

There was another flutter in 1818 when they initially resolved to bring a New River water supply to the houses, but the Company's estimate of 6 guineas a year per house, minimum 20 houses, was refused as too steep. In 1826 the water controversy came up again, when complaints were made of the dusty road in dry seasons — always a consideration in days before road metalling — and negotiations were renewed with the Company, this time for watering the Terrace road and the cross road to Highbury Place over the fields. At five shillings per 100 yards this worked out at more than £1 per house, and after great arguments, warnings that in case of fire they must send to Highbury Sluice House, $1\frac{1}{2}$ miles away, and alternative emergency offers of Mr Edward Wigan's leather bucket kept in his hall at no. 9, and Mr Henry Peto's stable pump from no. 4, they attempted a season with a hand watering-cart. Two months later they were happy to ask the Company for a water supply, with "a plug or two" for road watering.

Water supply at this date (it appears to have been installed by Michaelmas) was a limited service. The Company's terms, including a supply in case of fire, were now a mere 3 guineas a year per house, more for the larger houses; but water was only turned on for two hours three days a week, nor could the emergency fire supply be guaranteed because of the terrace's remote situation, on top of rising ground. Nevertheless the residents accepted.

By arrangement with Mr Robert Oldershaw, the Vestry Clerk, they had been enabled to keep on their private watchmen and lighting, under stricter regulations, with a corresponding rebate from the parish (1822). This ran into trouble when in 1824 they became interested in gas lighting, and made overtures to the parish for a supply. After some negotiation the lamps were installed in October 1825, 50 yards apart, at £3 apiece for posts and fittings and charged at 5 guineas a quarter. At once the residents decided that they needed more, and demanded four more lamps. Unfortunately it did not occur to them that this would mean an extra charge, and in 1832 they were incensed to receive Mr Oldershaw's demand for £54.14s for additional supply and maintenance. Having got away with it during the interval, and the parish Trustees having evidently overlooked it so far, the residents saw no reason to pay now. Their show of defiance and threat to have the extra lamps removed cut no ice with Oldershaw, who informed them laconically that if they wanted to reduce the lighting they could pay for the removal themselves. The Terrace tried bluff, offering half the arrears and refusing extra payment for the future. Oldershaw retaliated by having the four disputed lights extinguished. The Terrace capitulated.

Despite the occasional flurry of meetings, few inhabitants (and no ladies) attended meetings in person, several sending proxy votes even during the parish rating controversy. By the end of the minute-book (June 1834) only three members are turning up. The scope of committee duties must now have been much reduced, with the parish taking over most services, and like many local societies, it evidently tailed off with passing years and departing members. Mr William Cole, who unusually served as Treasurer for three years in succession, moved from no. 8 in July 1834, and their activities may well have then died away. By degrees they were being brought from their independent ways into a life-style more in line with the present day. Developments since their association first formed had been almost revolutionary. Nevertheless the antics of this early action group seem remarkably familiar.

John Spencer Square (1963)

John Spencer Square formed part of Canonbury rebuilding in the decades after the Second World War, by the developers Western Ground Rents. Streets renewed or restored included St Mary's Grove and Grange Grove, and Prior Bolton Street facing the open south side of this new 'square'.

It is really a square turned inside out — linked brick blocks of flat-roofed apartments, three storeys and stuccoed semi-basement, with central entrances, villa-style, approached by staircase bridges. It is ranged round three sides of a communal garden entered by similar back entrances in a minor key. Some of the trees are quite mature, and the general effect, if rather bland, is pleasant.

The architect was Western Ground Rents' surveyor Nash, who had also rebuilt part of the north side of Canonbury Square (q.v.).

Distinguished residents have included Baron Edward ('Ted') Castle, journalist and Alderman of the former GLC (d. 1979), and his wife the Rt Hon. Barbara Castle, PC, one-time Cabinet Minister and Leader of the Labour Group of the European Parliament.

Lonsdale Square (1838–45)

The land known as Gosseyfield immediately north of the Milner-Gibson estate was held of Barnsbury Manor by the Drapers' Company, to whom it was bequeathed in 1690 by the daughter of John Walter, one of its former Clerks. Its revenues were to

Lonsdale Square in 1938
Seen in its unreclaimed state. Designed by Richard Cromwell Carpenter for the
Drapers' Company, 1838, completed 1845

be used towards maintaining almshouses which Walter had founded in Southwark and Newington. The area long remained in rural use, and like many fields round Islington, in 1818 Gosseyfield is recorded as used for a cattle-pen for herds bound to and from Smithfield.

The Drapers' Company were relatively late in entering the building race, when the Milner-Gibson estate was all but complete. As architect they appointed their own surveyor, who was also district surveyor for East Islington. This was the young Richard Cromwell Carpenter (1812–55), friend of Pugin and a keen gothicist; he later designed several Gothic churches, including Lancing College Chapel. Carpenter's Lonsdale Square is Islington's – if not London's – sole Gothic venture in this genre, and in view of the Draper's Company's connections he possibly had in mind the newly fashionable Tudor almshouse style.

The single square which Gosseyfield could accommodate was laid out in 1838, not occupied until late 1842 and completed only in 1845. It is certainly an architectural curiosity, with rows of Tudor gables like some extended manor house; furthermore it is a rare example for Islington of a square designed *in toto* in uniform style (*pace* Milner Square).

The square is entered only from the centre of the north and south sides, on the north centred on the handsomely Italianate Drapers' Arms in Barnsbury Street; the south, looking down Stonefield Street into Cloudesley Square, is rather, *un*centred on Barry's Holy Trinity Church (q.v.).

The houses, like those of the surrounding area, were predominantly comfortable middle-class: in 1851 a third of the occupants were recorded as being in orders – perhaps the ecclesiastical style had appeal – and more than 14 per cent as professional. Occupation averaged 4–5 persons per household, including of course a servant.

The square's history was standard for Islington. It sank in prosperity early in the 20th century, the houses falling into multiple occupation, many let as furnished rooms, while the general fabric decayed. During the Second World War the railings were removed, but unlike most Islington squares the gardens remained privately owned, and a gardener was employed until 1959.

However, after vandalisation, breaking down of fences, and continued parking by heavy lorries, the Company offered the gardens freehold to the Council for a nominal £50, though a long time was to pass before improvements were made. In 1970/71 the Council replaced the unsightly chain-link fences by proper railings.

In 1954 the Drapers' Company auctioned the square, and when it had partly passed to private ownership the estate agents, Prebbles, who as Redspring were investing widely locally, acquired Stonesfield and Lonsdale property. Some 40 unprotected tenants in the square, mostly in single furnished rooms, were given notice. A Tenants' Crusade was then formed with the object of boycotting the agents unless houses were offered to sitting tenants.

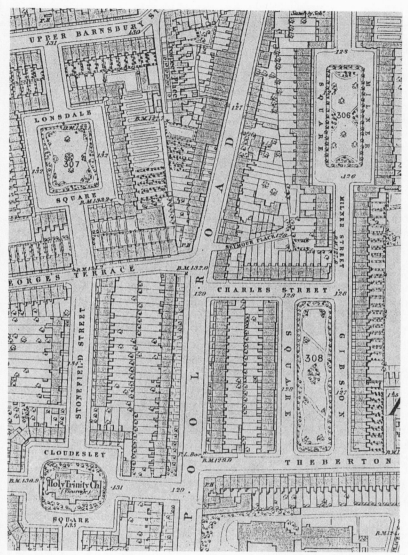

Lonsdale and Cloudesley Squares and the Milner-Gibson estate, 1871

Like other Islington squares, Lonsdale Square subsequently became owner-occupied. Many of the houses were converted into flats, and a general restoration took place. There is now an established residents' association.

Architecture
The style is harmonious if eccentric, and the layout symmetrical, the north and south entries each having five houses on either side. The houses are three storeys plus basements, and attics in the gables. No flat fronts here, but bays with high mullioned windows and Tudor arches over the front doors, lit by triple quatrefoils in place of the more orthodox fanlights. Careful scrutiny shows the sides as not quite equal, east and west sides of 14 houses each being slightly longer, though their houses are narrower. North and sides contain disproportionately fewer houses, the difference appearing in their having 4-pane bays and double windows between, while the longer sides' are three-pane (though *not* on the NW range).

In limiting entrances to the square to the centres of two sides the architect set himself a thorny problem – what to do with the corners. In some squares, e.g. Milner, the angle houses lie along the adjoining side; in others, e.g. Granville in Clerkenwell, the houses are simply built at right angles, meeting only at their front corner. Here, Carpenter squeezed out his corner houses behind the rest in lozengy form, grouping three front doors – of the corner house and the two flanking – in a hexagonal re-entrant. (The SW corner was left unbuilt, as garden ground, until the 1970s.)

The general effect is picturesque if not altogether happy, and the lofty, ecclesiastical-looking houses contain rather small rooms. The impression is rather of a series of over-blown almshouses, and as a domestic style it is hardly surprising that it did not catch on.

Inhabitants
Probably the most distinguished inhabitant was the prolific and versatile London journalist "Aleph", alias William Harvey, who died at no. 48 in 1873. He was a contributor to the London City Press and author of *London Scenes and London People* (1863); he was also a surgeon, and Honorary Superintendent of Islington Reformatory.

Another popular Victorian journalist resident was George Sims, son of a plate glass merchant in Aldersgate, born in Clerkenwell in 1847 and from the 1870s working on the *Weekly Despatch* and other papers, and author of a number of successful plays. In 1878–9 he was living at 30 Lonsdale Square, but by 1880 had moved to Camden Road and later still lived in Gower Street.

No. 3, Lonsdale House, was occupied in 1843–63 by one of Islington's many Academies for Young Gentlemen, run by Daniel Spranze, who had formerly kept a school in White Conduit Fields (later part of Barnsbury Road).

Malvern Terrace (1836)

Islington was prolific in nurseries for the young – not only "academies" for young ladies and gentlemen, but nursery gardens. Nelson, while remarking in 1811 that their number had lately "considerably diminished", still lists half a dozen totalling 34 acres, of which the distant Barr's at Ball's Pond was much the largest. Some of the smaller were in the Back Road area, where Mr Townsend had five acres between Islington Park Street and Barnsbury Street, a relic of the large grounds once owned by Jacob Harvey, JP, who had died in 1770 (pp. 112–3 and n.). Tiny pockets of this nursery still survived behind houses on either side of Barnsbury Street at the time of the first Ordnance Survey in 1871. Farther west, Mr Smith owned another nursery near Oldfield's dairy, and in 1835 when builders threatened to overrun the whole hill-top, Cromwell comments that "Mr Smith, and others of Liverpool Road" had acquired part of the former Albion Cricket-Ground for nurseries "lately formed at the south end" of the Thornhill estate (p. 398). His gloomy prediction that they too would soon be swallowed up by housing proved in one case to have a happier – and more complicated – outcome.

Malvern Terrace and Malvern Cottages, two short rows of linked cottages with large front gardens, were indeed built by December 1836 alongside the nursery's north boundary, separated by a plot on which James Hillman, perhaps one of the proprietors, had a shed and greenhouse, and apparently a tiny house. There were several greenhouses in the nursery, the one attached to Hillman's effectively separating the two new rows, so that Malvern Terrace was approached by a path across the gardens from what later became Richmond Avenue, and Malvern Cottages by a cobbled lane from Thornhill Road. Already in 1838 two other little houses flanked Hillman's tiny cot, filling the narrow gap with the present no. 6 (2-bay), no. 7 (1-bay – Hillman's) and no. 8 (2-bay), all minute even compared with their modest neighbours. Although Hillman's name is in the Rate Books, in the Directories it is the Smiths, first George and from 1867 John, presumably George's son.

Much of the nursery disappeared with the building of Richmond Crescent in 1852, but under John Smith as nurseryman four-fifths survived until 1889 (he appears to have died in 1890). The grounds were then taken over by the Vestry for a small public park, re-named Thornhill Gardens. They were included among gardens protected from building under the London Squares and Enclosures (Preservation) Act 1906, and have continued to be maintained by the Council.

With the creation of Thornhill Gardens and removal of the glasshouses, it was possible to run the narrow lane the full extent of the two rows.

Malvern Cottages in the 1889 directory is described as a "continuation of Malvern Terrace to Thornhill Road", and in 1890 was renumbered as part of the

Malvern Terrace in 1953
Built 1836 as two short rows of cottages adjoining a nursery garden (now
Thornhill Gardens). The unrestored terrace after World War II, with neglected
front gardens, showed little of its present-day charm

terrace. It has remained a cul-de-sac, ending on the west with the walls bordering
Richmond Crescent. Numbering starts from the closed end.

Architecture
No. 1, rather oddly, is a double-fronted 3-storey Victorian villa of the ?1850s, with
rusticated quoins and a central porch. The terrace proper, nos. 2–11, consists of 10
low two-storey linked villas, all double-fronted except for the central rhythm 2-1-2
of nos. 6–8. These three are further out of step with the placing of their cill-bands,
and no. 8's first-floor windows are rather grandly lengthened to floor level. All
ground-floor windows are circular-headed. There appear to have been few alterations apart from the front door and windows of no. 11. None of the houses have
astragals – and perhaps never had?

In Thornhill gardens are some fine mature trees. The cottage-terrace effect is one
of great charm, a rural retreat with its long front gardens, looking as if it should be
tucked into some corner of a village, and the street is still cobbled. It now has a local
fame for its annual street-party and opening of the gardens.

Milner Square (1841–7)
(See also Gibson Square)

Milner Square, although planned in some form among Islington's earliest estate developments, eventually took shape as one of its later squares. In his original plan for the Milner-Gibson estate (1824), Francis Edwards allotted the name to what was actually to be built as Gibson Square, while for the northern leg of the awkwardly-shaped estate he proposed a pair of widely spaced terraces. His revised plan of 1828 still shows the site as terraces, and it is still not allotted the name Milner.

Dove Brothers appear to have been briefed for the site as early as 1827, but it was not yet to include Milner Square. The delay was possibly for financial reasons. Francis Edwards now drops out of the picture, and only in 1839, when Gibson Square's east side was complete, is a plan submitted to the Holborn and Finsbury Commissioners for Sewers. This was made by the builder William Spencer Dove, who was then living on the new estate at 3 Trinidad Place (now 86 Liverpool Road), and it was for "The New Buildings proposed to be erected on the vacant ground between the north end of Gibson Square and Barnsbury Street", to be "of uniform architectural character throughout". "Those receding in the center will be upon a raised terrace, with Gardens on each side of the road", leaving a space of some 160 feet between; the advanced "wings" were to be brought forward to the street-line. Even then the new creation was styled "Milner Terrace", being as Dove put it, "a wide street narrowing on the north and south, rather than a square". Islington Proprietary School had already been built on its NE exit and Barnsbury Chapel on the NW.

No explanation appears to survive for the dropping of Edwards or the taking over by the two young architect partners, Alexander Dick Gough (1804–71) and Robert Lewis Roumieu (1814–77). They had been fellow-pupils under Benjamin Wyatt and had recently completed Islington Literary and Scientific Institution in Wellington Street (now Almeida Street), whose spare angular lines proved a foretaste of their other work in Islington. The Huguenot-descended Roumieu was the more original by far, and his influence, if not his actual design, can be detected in various houses in the area. The north side of Theberton Street (nos. 20–44) is probably by this pair.

In 1840 work began on the link with Gibson Square, Milner Street (now Milner Place), and in 1841 Milner Square's east side was begun. The next developments are hypothetical. The architects exhibited a drawing of the square (details unrecorded) at the Royal Academy in 1842, when according to the Sewer Rate Books only 14 houses were yet built. Dove the builder had now moved into one of these, no. 4 (he later moved to no. 7, then to no. 20). The whole east side, 25 houses, was completed only in 1844. Samuel Lewis, who in his *History of Islington* (1842) describes the square as "rapidly progressing", expresses as fact what must have rather been a pious hope, echoing Dove's 1839 description: "a handsome collection of 50 houses . . . an 'oblong' form and comprises, on each side of the road, a range of 25 houses . . . of which the 17 central ones are upon a raised terrace, set back 50 feet from the main road, and have a raised garden in front". In fact the west side was only begun in 1846.

Explanation for the long delay may lie in Roumieu's proposal for a handsome Greek-style church for the centre of the west side, as shown in his, unfortunately undated, drawing, "Design for the Exterior of a New Church or Chapel of Ease for St Mary's District, Islington, proposed to be erected in . . . the west side of Milner Square, immediately opposite and corresponding in every particular with those [buildings] already built forming the east side of the same." Its frontage was to be 60 feet and accommodation 1,000 congregation.

Still in 1847, according to the Post Office Directory, only the south-western range was built, and the square must have stood unfinished while the fate of the proposed church was decided. Islington had been given three new churches in 1839, St Stephen's, Canonbury, All Saints, Battle Bridge, and St James's, Chillingworth Road, and apart from Christ Church, Highbury (1846) no more churches were built in the parish until the 1850s. In view of the anxiety of the vicar, the Revd Daniel Wilson, about the Anglican church's failure to keep abreast of the rapidly increasing population, non-building of the Milner Square church is puzzling. It may have been due to lack of funds, or even to the proposed edifice's more than slightly unorthodox style.

For whatever reason, it did not materialise, and a churchless west side of the square was eventually completed as a replica of the east.

One oddity about the square's layout was dictated by its siting behind Dr Pitcairn's botanic garden, so that it could not be entered by road from the side nearest Upper Street. At no. 20 the place of the front door is taken by a passage through Wellington Place, with no. 20's door opening into it.

Like Gibson Square and the rest of south Islington, towards the end of the century Milner Square fell on evil days, and by the 1930s it was largely tenemented. The LCC did a maintenance job, stripping the (doubtless decayed) pilasters from doorcases and window surrounds and removing the heavy balustraded cornice which overshadowed the ground floor rooms. In 1936 Dove Brothers adapted the NE angle as a factory for the British Siphon Company, a change in keeping with Islington's making over at that time of many residential streets and houses to industry.

But Milner Square never fails to have a staggering effect. Christopher Hussey saw its positive side in 1939 (*Country Life*, 4 March, pp. 224–8): "most remarkable of the Barnsbury squares", "surprising", of "monumental" unity and "remarkable plastic quality". To Sir John Summerson, however, writing in *Georgian London* (1945 edition, p. 268), it was an object of horror: "perfectly extraordinary . . . most sinister . . . unreal and tortured", which whenever he saw it affected him like a recurring "unhappy dream".

By the 1950s the effect was of unrelieved gloom, and only in 1975 was the whole taken in hand by Islington Council, given a complete face-lift and subdivided into

Roumieu's proposed church for Milner Square

Milner Square, the NE corner in 1939
Nos. 1-4 were restored in the 1980s with restitution of missing features

Council flats. The overhanging features were not replaced except on nos. 1–4, but in other respects the external restoration has helped to recover much of the grandeur of the square's original impression.

Architecture
The square of 52 houses is conceived as a complete entity, with none of the differentiation between houses usually found in squares. The differentiation appears in the shape of the square itself, its duplicated corners and rounded angles. The houses, though not unduly narrow, seem so from their extraordinary verticality, which is the dominating impression in spite of the heavy horizontals intended to balance it.

The houses are tall, four storeys and basement, and not a single chimney stack breaks the relentless horizontal of the skyline. Roumieu's church drawing shows that he envisaged small pediments, presumably ranging all round the square, which would have introduced another dimension, perhaps not to happy effect – exchanging the danger of monotony for that of restlessness. The square might have been less overpowering had there been wider space available for the central garden, and the sides been set farther apart; but the site was, as we have seen, limited.

All features are rectangular except on the top floor, and all windows have lying panes. The first-floor windows extend to floor level. All are enclosed between narrow brick pilasters, again except for the top floor above its heavy cornice, like a running arcade alternating round-headed windows and blind windows. To-day, since the Council restoration, the effect is Venetian rather than neo-classical. Roumieu's drawing shows the shallow pilastered porticoes and window surrounds, and the balustrades intended at first-floor level, but the only places where these now appear are at nos. 1–4, a 1970s reconstruction, which otherwise exactly repeats the rest of the square.

The Milner Place houses, a kind of vestibule to the square and already caught up into its style, have ground floors in grooved stucco, with narrow round-headed doorways and windows, triple windows on the upper floors and a heavy cornice; only small attics, though again, as on the north side of Gibson Square, tall stacks suggest that a full-sized top floor was intended. On the west side, the return south wall of no. 7 picks up the square's verticality, with brick pilasters and stucco 'transom' effect. One enters the square via a duplicated angle at nos. 23–25 (E) and 26–28 (W).

At the north exit – still styled 'Milner Square' – the corner houses again continue round (nos. 1–3, 48–50). On the W side Barnsbury Chapel (1835–41) was in use until 1931, when it became Richford's Ironworks, unfortunately demolished in 1971. Flats built on the site by Kenneth Pring, with a brick 'bastion' at the rear in Barnsbury Street, recall some of the old chapel's angular features.

On the E side from 1830 Islington Proprietary School, later known as Islington High School, was closed in 1897 and converted to industrial use. It ended as a

Barnsbury Chapel, Barnsbury Street, in 1849
At the NW exit to Milner Square. Later used as an iron foundry and demolished
in 1971, replaced by flats

greetings card factory, and was regrettably demolished in 1984. The building, with
Gothic overtones, had had a further storey added, but retained its 'Perpendicular'
porch with ornately pinnacled pediment, crowned by the legend *Lac caseus infans* –
"Good milk, young cheese", a reference to Islington's nearby dairies but of obscure
relevance. Its replacement in 1987 by Waterloo Gardens by Christopher Libby
retains the pediment and inscription, re-erected on the Barnsbury Street front. The
impressive block of offices and flats, with arcaded ground floor, has latticed balconies
above giving a gaily Mediterranean effect, set between windows in tall brick sunk
panels. Large stone balls – a Libby 'trade-mark' – punctuate the unequally sized
arches at ground level, ending with an entry through to the back court. One feels that
Roumieu might have approved.

Inhabitants
The square has been hardly more blessed with famous inhabitants than has Gibson
Square. Its builder, William Spencer Dove, lived at three of its houses, nos. 4, 7 and
20, presumably camping in each until another was finished. Alexander Kennedy
Isbister (1822–83), teacher and educational author, died at no. 20 on 28 May 1883,

having been master at the Proprietary School (1849–55), later Headmaster of the Jews' College in Finsbury Square (1856–8), and Master of the Stationers' Company School (1858–62); also Dean of the College of Preceptors from 1872 until his death.

At 7 Milner Place (then Milner Street) from 1877–1905 lived George Rutter Fletcher, FSA, solicitor and antiquary, father of the artist Hanslip Fletcher (1874–1955), and grandfather of Geoffrey Fletcher. G. R. Fletcher's wife, daughter of a surgeon, Thomas Hanslip, earlier lived in the same house.

Packington Square (1966–70)

The saga of the Packington estate in the 1960s and 1970s was important in the history of public attitudes to conservation and rehabilitation. The story starts in 1960, when the City Parochial Foundation, then owners of that part of the former Clothworkers' estate, sold to Ve-Ri-Best Manufacturing Company. This firm drew up a pilot rebuilding proposal which, to general dismay, would dispossess many tenants unprotected since the 1957 Rent Act. Islington Council intervened with the threat of a CPO on the properties, but eventually, after negotiation, purchased the whole estate (1963).

A large-scale Council improvement plan was then proposed to modernise about 200 houses in eight streets: Arlington Avenue, Bevan, Dame, Packington, Prebend, Rector and St Paul Streets, and the east side of Union Square (q.v.). However, as the Government subsidy for a redevelopment scheme seemed better from the ratepayers' point of view, on the advice of the Ministry of Housing and Local Government the Council substituted a £2-million plan for total rebuilding of the $22\frac{1}{2}$-acre site. They commissioned Harry Moncrieff of Co-operative Planning Ltd – his largest undertaking to date – who produced a scheme for 540 dwellings in six-storey flatted blocks made from precast concrete units, and linked by walkways, with underground parking. The work was planned in two stages, with temporary re-housing for those first moved out.

This scheme, which meant wholesale demolition of the area, aroused strong public objections. The tenants formed a residents' association, many organisations registered strong disapproval at the destruction of potentially reclaimable terraced Victorian houses with gardens, and in 1965, when the LCC ended its existence under local government reform, the argument was still unresolved. The Council decided to treat this as a 'deemed refusal', and appealed to the Labour Minister for Housing and Local Government, Richard Crossman.

A prolonged public enquiry followed. The Packington estate was seen as a splendid opportunity for urban renewal by creating a modern, attractive, economic housing complex, and the inevitable arguments were advanced in its favour: that the 1850s houses had small architectural merit and their layout none at all, and that

Packington Street, after bomb damage in World War II
This and neighbouring streets on the 1850s Packington estate were
demolished by Islington Council to build Packington Square

retention was unsuitable because of poor construction and years of neglect. The houses were described as shoddy, lacking plumbing and essential services, and sagging because of weak foundations built directly on London clay. They were, it was claimed, beyond redemption.

Rehabilitation advocates, in addition to the usual conservation arguments, objected to the extra cost of rebuilding – £2 as opposed to £1¼ million for restoration – and pointed out that Islington had pockets of far worse housing, notably Beaconsfield Buildings or "The Crumbles", whose continued existence was a disgrace. Supporters of this view included, besides many residents, the new GLC, the Civic Trust, London & Manchester Assurance Co. (former owners of the estate), and local amenity societies, notably the Islington Society.

Islington authorities were accused of making decisions in private before formally passing them in Council, and a small group of councillors rebelled against the official line. But already the Council were beginning to evacuate the Packington houses, and by degrees the area was run down.

The case, which drew national publicity, was further bedevilled by the current GLC intention – subsequently abandoned – to build a three-lane motorway along-side the Regent's Canal by Arlington Avenue, as part of the contemporary belief that the Angel traffic problem could be solved by urban motorways, underpasses and flyovers.

The Inspector at the public inquiry, Mr D. I. Pryde, recommended approval of the rebuilding plan, but the Minister expressed dissatisfaction with the scheme and, overriding his decision, refused planning consent, while leaving it open for the plan to be revised (July 1965). This seemed good news for the conservationists, but in September it proved that the Minister had now decided against rehabilitation, and was concerned only with the quality of the new scheme. Harry Moncrieff's plan was re-submitted with amendments, and was accepted.

There was strong criticism of Mr Crossman both in and out of Parliament for failing to consult the objectors on this renewed application. The Minister protested that it had been "a finely balanced decision" between the need for enquiry and the dangers of further delay. A demand for a renewed enquiry was refused by the Lord Chancellor. Islington Council published a bulletin maintaining that renewed representation had not been invited because the Minister was "no longer interested" in rehabilitation, and that "no competent professional adviser or consultant" had differed from their own preference for rebuilding. This was attacked as untrue, and the statement was withdrawn. The Minister now argued that the old houses were not good – the standard claim in these cases – coupled with the rather inconsistent theory that, were they restored, "a sort of little Canonbury" would result and the original working-class tenants be squeezed out. He did, however, on an Opposition censure motion, apologise to the Council on Tribunals, which was investigating the objectors' complaints of mal-administration, for apparent discourtesy over his handling of the case.

The objectors scored one victory: the GLC promised to acquire and demolish "The Crumbles".

The amended Moncrieff plan, accepted by the Minister in November, was similar to the first except in detail, and would rehouse 1,632 residents in 539 dwellings, 12 flats to a house. The expected completion time was $2\frac{1}{2}$ years, but already the scheme had been delayed by a year, and there was further delay while permission was secured for the necessary road closures during building. The whole area was blighted and the houses became derelict and vandalised. By June 1966 only a single inhabitant remained, in Arlington Avenue.

Additional costs of £350,000 were now announced, the result of rising prices and taxes, and of work required above the estimate. This was now nearly £$2\frac{1}{2}$ million, excluding salaries, and fees to architects and surveyors. Nevertheless, the Minister had approved of the quality of the project, held to be Greater London's most expensive ever for council flats. It was also Islington Council's largest undertaking to date, and its first use of the modern industrial system by which the builders, Wates Construction Ltd, erected two temporary factories to manufacture the precast components – walls, floors, staircases – on site.

Work started in May 1967, after further setbacks and met with expected and unexpected difficulties: disgruntled inhabitants, noisy guard dogs, non-stop pile-drivers, a "Berlin Wall" that cut off one part of the estate from the rest. Some 16 months later, however, 88 flats were finished and occupied, 208 more almost ready. The whole estate was complete by August, 1970.

The promised amenities included play spaces instead of individual gardens; traffic-free 'squares', and the surrounding roads closed to cars; footbridges over Packington Street and access to flats by upper floors; balconies; central heating systems; fitted equipment for all flats such as built-in wardrobes.

The object had been to 'create' a community atmosphere (a popular wish-fulfilment dream of the time), to maintain the local building scale (but in fact the blocks were noticeably higher than surrounding houses), and to provide parking (but only half the residents were provided for). Harry Brack, one of the 'rebel councillors', who had been expelled from the local Labour Party for his Packington views, complained bitterly in an *Evening Standard* article (18 September, 1969) of the glaring contrast between intention and reality, between the pleasant, quiet remnant of Union Square and the "ten huge liver-sausage-coloured concrete slabs" of the new buildings, "impersonal, rigid and monotonous".

Not all shared his views, and many tenants enjoyed their luxurious new facilities. But reception was mixed: some found the play area too small, the promised football pitches had been dropped, and the rents, rates and garden charges were more than they could afford. Councillors, however, spoke admiringly of Packington's inspiration from "Georgian squares" . . . apart from their scale, height, skyline, and so on.

Difficulties proved to be more than teething troubles. According to the Tenants' Association recreation facilities were overloaded, and after a few years there were tales of rival gangs. The press made much of the Packington "jungle", or residents' fear of going out at night, the trouble caused by the street bridges, which had to be closed, the lack of social amenities, and juvenile delinquency. Some families moved out, but those who stayed resented the press stigma, pointing out that clubs were being formed, that vandals would grow up, and younger siblings were quieter.

In the 1980s other problems surfaced: the youth centres could not keep up, the police considered Packington a black spot, there was new talk of "gang rule". On the practical side, the much-praised central heating boilers proved unsatisfactory and new individual heating had to be installed. In 1990 a year-long, £1-million face-lift was launched as the 1960s design was now seen as "disastrous" for security. New lift-shafts were installed, new entrances and lobbies with entry-phones, and the once fashionable walkways were blocked off. A "Packington Project" was formed to approach the youth problem positively by providing alternative interests. At Easter 1992 the Council opened a new community centre built on stilts in Packington Square, the DOE and the Safer Cities Project paying the cost of more than £$\frac{1}{2}$-million. It contained workshops for local businesses, meeting rooms and kitchens, and a patio above, and was to provide the much-needed facilities to tenants for recreation and socialising. Not long afterwards traders in the shopping mall, which had declined and lost customers, attempted without much success to boost trade by a Saturday market, and in the summer the Council made a plea for a grant from the Department of the Environment under the economic regeneration scheme.

Had the opportunity to develop the Packington estate come only a few years later, the decision would probably have been to rehabilitate rather than sweep away the long established residential area and its existing community atmosphere. Paradoxically, however, it was the Packington experience which has contributed largely to changing attitudes in conservation. Losing the Packington battle contributed towards winning the war.

Architecture

The name Packington Square partly recalls the half-demolished Union Square on which one end of it encroached; and it has certain affinities with Peabody Square – in layout as well as in the noble aspiration behind which realisation often lags. The top end of the complex of flatted blocks, abutting on Union Square's NW corner, is bounded by Rector, Prebend and Packington Streets, the last being the main vehicle entrance and parking access. This northern block forms three sides of an open square round a central recreational space, and a pedestrian way separates it from the rest. A notable decorative feature is the large concrete balls crowning pillars at the main entrance.,

The remainder of the estate, whose north side forms as it were a detached side of Packington Square, continues at right angles to it, in linked blocks or open squares, as far as the canal, here crossed by the estate's own pedestrian bridge. Some ranges have continuous balconies forming the walkways, under a sloping glass canopy. Whatever its deficiencies, it was an improvement on tower blocks.

Peabody Square (1866)

George Peabody, merchant banker and philanthropist, who by his own efforts became rich and successful, was an American born in Massachusetts in 1795 of poor parents. He lived in London from 1837 until his death in 1869, and in 1862, by a gift of £150,000 to form the Peabody Donation Fund towards the building of housing for the poor (later increased to £$\frac{1}{2}$-million), he initiated what was to become London's largest housing trust.

Peabody Square, with Peabody House, in Greenman Street, was the second such tenement to be erected after the original pattern by H. A. Darbishire, in 1866. It was the earliest attempt in Islington to provide proper housing for the working class in place of its worst slums. The object was to create cheap, clean and properly drained

Peabody Square (1866), Greenman Street, looking SW
An early estate financed by the American philanthropist George Peabody.
The central monument was probably never built. Tibberton Square is just off
the bottom of the picture.
From a contemporary lithograph

apartments, and although the building style was uncompromisingly dour, with grey brick walls, factory-like segmental windows, lowering eaves and heavy chimney-stacks, the amenities provided made the accommodation greatly sought-after as an escape from inhuman slums and rookeries.

After the Second World War new Peabody properties were built, and older blocks by degrees converted and modernised – Islington's in 1965. After the 1974 Housing Act, which gave official recognition to the voluntary sector in housing, the Donation Fund reverted to its original role as a general charity, continuing to administer the existing houses, while a housing association was formed to provide new buildings. In 1990 a general Estate Renewal Programme was launched, with the object of spending some $200 million on modernisation of the now ageing buildings over the coming decade.

The old paternalist approach has given way to one of more partnership with tenants, and a Community Fund finances wider-based community projects.

The site

The Greenman Street 'square' was built on the site of Ward's Place, popularly known as "King John's Place", and by a "vulgar tradition" (says Nelson) believed to be one of that King's palaces: a low, rambling building, part timber-framed, with a gable at one end and a wide bay at the other. Later it was probably occupied by Sir Robert Ducie, a Lord Mayor who died in 1634, and the initials HD over the door might have referred to his son, Sir Hugh. [VCH 14, 15, 103] In the 18th century it was rented by Dr Robert Poole as an inoculation hospital, and later became a branch of his Coldbath Fields Smallpox Hospital. From the 1760s it was used as a dissenters' chapel, then as the parish workhouse, and later still as a soap manufactory. It ended its days as a workmen's tenement, and was demolished in 1800. The immediate area became one of mean hovels and decaying cottages, including one called "Sun Row", and a maze of church schools and Ragged School buildings.

Peabody Buildings occupied a larger area than the site of this old mansion, and for its erection a number of other decaying tenements, such as Mary Row and Albert Place, were demolished. Many would have been the run-down cottages of ancillary craftsmen to the watch and clock trades, traditionally established in narrow streets off the Lower Road.

Architecture

The Buildings are four long, free-standing, five-storey blocks ranged round an open square. In the centre was placed a large clock-tower-style 'monument', since removed. The design adopted here, as in the other early Peabody estates such as Stamford Street, Lambeth (1875) and Shadwell (1886) might almost be termed 'college staircase' – each stair giving access to sets of rooms, in this case two or three flats. Each staircase had a cold-water sink and WC, and each block a communal laundry – model facilities for the time. All flats, ranging from one to four rooms, had a range for heating and cooking, a water-boiler, cupboards and a coal store. The 'square' plan, allowing for a central play space, was an improvement on the more cramped proto-example at Spitalfields, completed a year earlier.

A great improvement on current housing for its amenities, visually its massive slabs loomed menacingly over the low, often decaying housing of its surroundings. Grim and drab though the prison-like blocks appear, they have a certain dignity, and express vividly the philanthropy of their day.

Peckett Square, Taverner Square, Highbury Grange (1922)

These two series of flats, in the form of squares, are part of the former Addington Mansions flats, built on the site of several villas on the east side of Highbury Park and south side of Highbury Grange, and opened by the Mayor of Islington in July 1922. The ceremony is recorded on a now barely legible tablet on the E end of the main block, now called Matthews Court. The flats were named after Alderman Frederick John Addington, who served the Council until 1925 and was a long-time supporter of the Trade Union movement.

In 1977 modernisation began on the whole complex, and the result was renamed Taverner Estate, after Louis Taverner, land-owner in 1848 of much of the Highbury Grange property. The two square-like ends were also renamed, the eastern Taverner Square, rehabilitated 1979, the western Peckett Square, rehabilitated 1980/81. George Peckett, who lived at no. 10 (now no. 6) Aberdeen Park, had served on the Vestry 1861–6, and was on the Committee set up to establish Finsbury Park.

The 4-storey buildings are in red brick with stone dressings, e.g. the tall 'Queen Anne' keystones, and form a solidly reassuring frontage, on the Highbury Park side with projecting blocks, in Highbury Grange with shallow bays of alternating heights and contrasting shapes. The two 'squares' – Peckett Square has a later south addition – are ranged round central ornamental areas, with grass and now mature trees.

Thornhill Square (1847–9; 1851–2) and the Thornhill Estate

Thornhill Square is not only Islington's largest square, but for many years was one of its largest open spaces. The Thornhill estate, marching with Pentonville and extending downhill from the present Thornhill Road on the hill-top to what became the Caledonian or Chalk Road, was lowermost and most westerly of the Barnsbury manor estates, and among the last to remain in private hands.

The Thornhill family came originally from Yorkshire, and by the 18th century were land-owners in several counties, chiefly Huntingdonshire and Cambridgeshire. Their property near Islington, like most of the local land, was let for dairy farming,

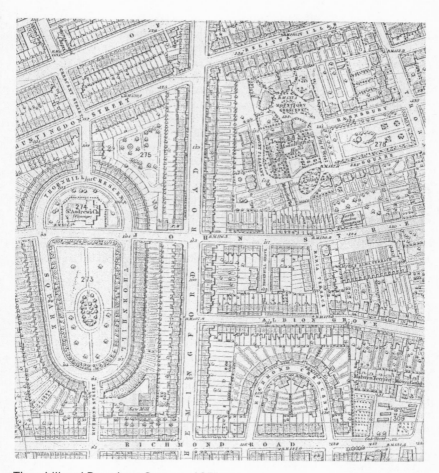

Thornhill and Barnsbury Squares, 1871
The 1871 Ordnance Survey also shows Malvern Terrace and Cottages, with
nursery gardens and glasshouses still in place; as are nos. 64 and 65 Thornhill
Square (site of Islington West Library), the sawmill in the SE quadrant behind
the square, and the then St Andrew's vicarage garden, now the semi-wild
Barnsbury Wood

though one tenant, Christopher Bartholomew, owned the White Conduit House and its gardens at the top of the hill. By the turn of the 19th century George Thornhill, the then owner, in old age saw his Islington estate as appropriate for development: he may have been influenced by John Dawes's enterprise in Canonbury, and had he succeeded in launching his big project when he first actively considered it (1808), the Thornhill estate would have been in the vanguard of Islington development.

George Thornhill, who was already 70, authorised a surveyor named Henry Richardson to draw up a building lease with William Horsfall, a neighbouring land-owner, but disagreements caused the plan to fall through in 1810 when they had got no further than planning a layout, including a crescent, and ordering the brick-making. Thornhill then turned instead to the 35-year-old Joseph Kay, surveyor to the Foundling Estate in Bloomsbury as successor to Samuel Pepys Cockerell, whose pupil he had been. Brick-making and discussions with Horsfall continued.

In 1812 the estate's potential was increased by its being on the route of the new Regent's Canal, of which Thornhill was one of the proprietors, and Kay and Horsfall were considering the line of a road across the estate which would bridge the canal.

The canal building made slow progress, however, and Thornhill's plans none at all. In 1820 the old gentleman made an elaborate will, which included a bequest of £12,000 in trust to his son George junior (b. 1783) and daughter-in-law for 'improvement' of the Islington estate, for by this time agricultural land in the area generally was beginning to give way to brick-fields, in anticipation of a building boom. But Mr Thornhill lived on until July 1827, and still there was no building development on his estate.

In 1823 the line was surveyed of a new 'Parliamentary' road to connect Battle Bridge with Holloway (i.e. the Caledonian Road): it passed through the western limit of Thornhill's land, and George Junior was a shareholder in the Battle Bridge and Holloway Road Company, active in the campaign for the Bill and in safeguarding the family interests. He was chairman of a committee of which Thomas Cubitt was a member, among the questions needing settlement being a toll-gate and a bridge over the canal (Thornhill bridge). The Bill for the road passed in 1825, though subsequent negotiations were still in progress when Thornhill senior died, leaving his son in charge of the estate. Under George junior's ownership Joseph Kay continued as manager until 1849.

The Thornhill estate papers, copious in documentation of the earlier period of discussion and delay, unfortunately dry up just at the more interesting time when building was actually going on, partly no doubt because Thornhill now became MP for Huntingdonshire and his personal interest was diverted.

Building made a very slow start in 1829, based on the estate street plan. At this stage only a single terrace materialised, the six houses of Gainford Terrace, now 76–86 Richmond Avenue. During the 1830s and 1840s the axial Hemingford Road, in parallel with the meandering Thornhill Road at the hill-top and the straight line of the new Caledonian Road below, was built up in parcels and in distinctly contrasting styles, first rated in 1848 and 1849. As usual in the development of a family estate, names for the new streets were derived from the family or from their lands, and among the assorted choices were Offord, Huntingdon, Hemingford, Matilda and Everilda.

The area was the fringe both of Islington parish and of London, and Caledonian Fields and Barnsbury Fields, stretching from the White Conduit site on the ridge down to the vale of Maiden Lane with its nuisance industries and the new Chalk Road, began poor and remained so: "little more than a mere waste, dotted with cottages, and with huts, as stunted in their proportions as the majority of their inmates were in moral character. The 'Fields' were generally of that low cast which is common upon the borders of an overgrown city." So did the early 1840s appear from the smug viewpoint of the *Illustrated London News* in 1854, by which time the Thornhill estate was built up and its new St Andrew's Church consecrated. West Barnsbury, adjoining the estate, was run up in little streets and terraces of small cottages, jerry-built for the underpaid, underprivileged and sickly, in the area between Pentonville and Copenhagen Street. It bordered the entrance to the new Regent's Canal tunnel and extended along either side of the water. (Much of this was to be demolished in the 1930s and after the war, especially in the 1980s, replaced by Council estates obliterating most of the street pattern.) First the building of the Model Prison called Pentonville (1841) began to scare away the degraded population, then "the cottages and huts were swept away, and houses for the respectable classes were built upon the sites of that wretched rurality." Not far off, on the hilly fields surrounding old Copenhagen House and its pleasure grounds, the new cattle market was shortly to open, replacing Smithfield which was at last closed in 1855.

Building in the square appears to have started in 1847, when G. S. S. Williams produced 33 houses on the west side; by 1849 quadrant and crescent were under way, the latter by Samuel Pocock of the dairy-farm family, and completion was in 1852 — 44 years after the project was first discussed.

Within the south-east quadrant a large enclosed space became a minor echo of the larger enclosure that was to become Barnsbury Wood (see p. 145). Whereas in the south-west quadrant this was filled with spacious gardens, on the south east Williams, who was living at 3 Richmond Street (now Matilda Street), and by 1852 was living at 32 Thornhill Square, set up a builder's work-yard. The area bounded by the quadrant, Hemingford Road and Richmond Avenue, became filled over several decades with industrial buildings, hidden from the roads by high walls and timber gates. They remained *in situ* until the summer of 1992, notably a tall chimney of octagonal bricks, which may have been contemporary with the square or was perhaps rebuilt *c.* 1870. They were then dismantled for the building of a small residential complex, but a preservation order was placed on the picturesque chimney, in spite of which it was then demolished.

The Square and St Andrew's Church

Thornhill Square, so called, is characteristic of Islington in being not a square at all. It is an ellipse, ovoid rather, with the wider end to the north, and may be read as two crescents bounding a 'square' with only two built sides. There are as usual other anomalies. The layout is not quite symmetrical, Bridgeman Road, the chord of the arc, cutting across not quite at right angles, so that the NW quadrant of the crescent has one house more than the NE. The parallel roads on the estate boundary, Huntingdon Street and Offord Road, similarly make an acute angle with Hemingford Road, resulting in that other anomaly, Barnsbury Wood (q.v.).

In the crescent gardens in 1852–4 was built the cruciform St Andrew's Church, its design chosen by competition and won by the architects Francis Newman and John Johnson. Newman is known only for an unsuccessful design for the Crystal Palace, but Johnson, a winner of both silver and gold medals when a student at the Royal Academy, was the designer of sumptuous Italianate houses and of churches in the 'Decorated' style. He favoured Kentish rag with ashlar dressings for materials, and a tower and spire, high-pitched roofs and buttresses, all employed at St Andrew's. Not surprisingly the cost exceeded the sum prudently stated in the competition conditions, with the vain hope of keeping down expenses.

The decision to create a new church district had been taken at two parish meetings, in order to relieve the ever overburdened parish of St Mary's. It was to supplement the already crowded districts of Holy Trinity, Cloudesley Square and All Saints, Caledonian Road, which could no longer cope with the population, now over 30,000 and still growing rapidly. St Andrew's, built by Dove Brothers, costing £6,500 and by far the largest of Islington's new churches, completed the move towards this area's respectability. George Thornhill, now an MP, offered not only the site but a £500 donation, and more modest donors included Samuel Pocock of the dairying family and builder of the crescent, who gave £100 for the railings, and Mr Wontner, builder of Tibberton Square, who gave a humble £2.

To consecrate so grand a building, in January 1854, no one less than the Bishop, Dr Charles Blomfield, would do, attended by the Lord Mayor, Thomas Sidney, and City dignitaries, even though on completion a debt of more than £2,000 was still outstanding.

So emerged Islington's largest and in some ways grandest residential enclosed space, and one of its last in Victorian times. Inhabitants of the new estate were well-to-do compared with, for example, those in Mr Henry Rydon's new houses round Arlington Square, and the area attracted lawyers, doctors, merchants and retired clergy as well as a few artists and singers.

In 1906 the two north-western houses of the square (nos. 64 and 65) were demolished to make way for a new West Library for the Borough. Its architect was E. Beresford Pite, a pupil of John Belcher and working much in the Arts and Crafts style.

St Andrew's Church, Thornhill Square
by Newman and Johnson (1852–4), in the north crescent of the elliptical
'square'
From a contemporary engraving

Otherwise the square has seen little architectural change apart from loss of a few features – notably window-heads – thanks to World War II and the wear and tear of decades. Yet after the war it was badly run down, and was one of the later areas of Barnsbury to be reclaimed and rehabilitated.

The district had been further sub-divided in 1862 by the building of St Thomas's Church off Hemingford Road, but on the latter's demolition in 1953 the districts were reunited, and from 1956 included the former St Matthias's in Caledonian Road and from 1980 Holy Trinity as well. A century after St Andrew's completion the population was steadily falling, though in 1959 still at least 25,000; and about a third of the property in the surrounding square mile was condemned for Council rebuilding, the vicar claiming that women were afraid to attend church on dark evenings because of the disagreeable neighbourhood.

After the death of the family representative, Captain Noel Thornhill, in 1955, the estate's future was uncertain. In 1960 parts were bought by John D. Wood & Co., and rumours of a break-up followed; but in 1970 99 per cent, including the crescent and square, was still owned by the Trustees of the Thornhill Estate. Eventually many of the freeholds were privately purchased by occupants, and the 1980s saw a marked revival in the visible prosperity of the square and its houses.

Architecture
The square is ringed with 63 houses (originally 65) incorporating the SW and SE quadrants, with another 33 houses in the crescent. The spare classical style seen in earlier squares had given way by the 1850s to heavy Roman detail, and the houses on the E and W sides have grooved stucco ground floors with segmental window heads, and front doors and first-floor windows with bracketed hoods adorned with rosettes. Beneath the stucco bracketed cornices a terrace rhythm of houses in sets is discernible, end and central houses slightly advanced, one bay instead of two, with tripartite first-floor windows and balconies and alternating triangular and segmental pediments. The windows of the other houses have simple hoods, and window-guards with anthemion motif within looped rails.

The crescent has simpler finishings, small pediments only in the end and central groups: it runs 3-4-4-4-2 in the NW quadrant (17 houses) and 2-4-3-4-3 in the NE (16 houses). Every third and fourth house have paired front doors (1-1-2-1-1-2, etc.). The blank end walls have been filled with blind windows (nos. 1, 17, 18), with the doors in side porticos; but no. 33, now the Buffalo Club, in the south crescent, has had a recent extension in well-matching pastiche. Less happy is its sign, to accommodate which one capital has been trimmed off. A few pediments have been lost (e.g. Bridgeman Road, which has alternating round and triangular).

All houses are three storey with basement – a few have later mansard attics – but although no less tall than in other squares, they appear so because of the width of open space between. The houses were built with conservatories at the rear, many of which remain.

The West Library (Beresford Pite, 1907)   Of two colours of brick, with stone dressings, surmounted by an octagon lantern. The windows are set in circular-headed blank arches with deep stone lintels, each with a carved letter of the alphabet in foliage. On the square side they are set singly between brick giant pilasters, the upper windows arched with triangular pediments on brackets. On the Bridgeman Road façade they are grouped together and the pediments form a continuous arcade, below a blind 'thermal' brick arch and crowning gable; brick relieving arches flank the windows on each floor. There is a lower West wing with a porch, and a single-floor extension.

In August 1992 the future of the building came under serious threat, when the library was the one condemned to closure under current Council spending cuts. It was subsequently reprieved.

St Andrew's Church   Cruciform was considered the appropriate shape for a church with so large a congregation as St Andrew's. The material was the fashionable Kentish rag, with dressed stone features including buttresses, and the style, as contemporaries liked to term it, "Middle Pointed", or quasi-13th century with an ogee-headed East window and some elaborate window tracery. The tower with broach spire was sited not at the crossing, as usual with a transeptal church, but at the W end of the south aisle. The *Ecclesiologist* of the time was disapproving: "An ostentatious cruciform pile, all gables and transepts, with an exaggerated broach".

Internally, West end galleries increased the available accommodation. The East gallery at first contained the organ, which was later moved to the west. Though the congregation in its heyday sometimes crowded to the doors, good acoustics ensured that they could hear the preacher from his Caen stone pulpit.

In the 1960s pews and pulpit were removed with the object — in the event unpopular with many parishioners — of integrating the church more with the community, and the interior was partitioned for various uses, including a school-room, kitchen and coffee room, quiet room and offices. In the 1980s the exterior of the church was extensively refurbished, to dramatic effect.

The Gardens, long enclosed by railings and, as with other squares, open only to key-holders, were Islington's largest (though private) recreational space until Highbury Fields were acquired in the 1880s. In 1946 Captain Thornhill handed the gardens over to the Council for public use, and they were opened by the Mayor in 1947. Their condition had become deplorable during the war, however, and only in 1953 were they newly laid out under the Council's Open Spaces scheme, as part of Coronation Year improvements. The effect is agreeably park-like, the skilful

Islington West Library, Thornhill Square in the 1940s
A distinguished building by E. Beresford Pite (1907), on the site of the two
end houses of the square

banking up of ground at the Bridgeman Road end creating a pleasant feeling of enclosure.

Barnsbury Wood

A remarkable, perhaps unique, feature of the land round Thornhill Square is the locally famous phenomenon of "Barnsbury Wood", an unusually large enclosure created by the sharp angle of Huntingdon Street, forming a space of about 0.86 acre behind the 61 houses of Hemingford Road, Huntingdon Street, Crescent Street and Thornhill Crescent. On the opposite (NW) side of the crescent only a 'normal'-sized garden patch was left. The larger space was originally allotted to the then vicarage at 7 Huntingdon Street, the biggest house in the row and backing directly on to it: the 1874 Ordnance Survey map shows paths and lawns, dotted with trees and shrubs. The vicarage later became a private school, and was subsequently divided into flats.

During the decay of the area the garden ran wild, and gradually reverted to woodland through natural growth, until by the 1960s it not only contained several mature trees but was a well-loved local asset. Any attempts to develop it were fiercely resisted, and in 1973 the Council stepped in after refusing planning permission to build to designs by Basil Spence; fortunately for the conservationists the difficulty of access, then and later, made building proposals impracticable. The Council, having bought the site for £$\frac{1}{2}$ million, had to drop its own housing plans, and found such problems over possible alternative uses that it was decided to leave the 'wood' in its semi-natural state, while helping with maintenance. To facilitate access nos. 1 and 2 Crescent Street were demolished.

In 1981 building again threatened, and a co-operative was formed by local residents with proposals to buy and manage the site. By then it had 74 trees, and was a habitat for ducks, jays, kestrels and the 'Barnsbury owls', claimed to be heard but never seen. There was also a flock of wood pigeons. Eventually the group was able to set up a scheme for running the wood as an ecological park.

It still maintains an air of mystery, and its apparent inaccessibility adds to the charm. Entry is available to schools, ecological groups and other local organisations, and passers-by gaze longingly at the secret enclosure through such cracks and knotholes as they can find.

Postscript

In *The Draper* of 16 July 1869 and for some time after, a Dr Barnes of 30 Thornhill Crescent ran an alluring advertisement for a cure-all for "the Nervous and Debilitated": a "wonderful medical guide ... the Secret Friend", illustrated by cases and testimonials and "Just published for 2 stamps" (post free). In it, he promised, was revealed the cause and cure of nervous debility, depression, timidity, pains in the back, impediments to marriage, venereal disease, "without the use of mercury".

Whether Dr Barnes felt particularly concerned for overworked drapers' assistants, on their feet for 12 hours a day – or how successful he was – is not revealed.

Tibberton Square (1827)

Tibberton Square is doubly an oddity: architecturally, having never had a fourth side, and historically, as the creation of one man for philanthropic reasons.

The originator was Thomas Wontner (1747–1831), who in 1771 moved from his native Herefordshire with his young wife and brother John to become an apprentice hatter in London, while John entered the watch and clock trade. In the year before their move, Thomas had married Margaret Lowe, a girl whom he first met at church in the village of Tibberton, in Worcestershire.

Both brothers later set up independently in the Minories, prospered, and were eventually joined in business by their sons. Thomas become a Freeman of the City, a Liveryman, and in 1793 Master of the Worshipful Company of Feltmakers, an office he was to fill again the year before his death. Of strong religious persuasion, he was for over 40 years (1782–1823) Manager and Controller of the Countess of Huntingdon's City chapel, in association with the reformer William Wilberforce, and was a founder of both the London Missionary Society and the British and Foreign Bible Society.

Wontner extended his hat-making works by opening a large fur manufactory in rural Islington, where he employed nearly 60 men and women for (says Nelson in his *History* of 1811, p. 199), "separating and sorting the hair of beaver, seal and other skins", ready for making into hats and other goods. The factory was near the foot of Green man's Lane (now Greenman Street), named after an old alehouse.

Next, Wontner built himself a family house with a large front garden near his new factory, and after living in the City for 37 years, moved there in 1808. In 1812 the New North Road, connecting Canonbury and the City, cut south across the Lower Road very near his factory and house, close to the eastern tip of St Mary's parish. Towards Ball's Pond, a little beyond the Lower Road intersection, in 1819 a few streets were built including Annett's Crescent. The rest was open country, and south of the fur factory stretched a space named Islington Common.

Wontner's wife died in 1823. Not long afterwards he decided to build houses on the garden in front of his villa. The area was irregular, rhomboid rather than rectangular, with the villa on the western edge near its top corner. The result was Tibberton Square, as Wontner nostalgically named it in memory of his first meeting with his beloved wife. It consisted of two east-west terraces of unequal length with a garden strip between, a couple of larger houses at the north-west corner because of the extra length on that side, and (apparently) four others linking with the villa to form the short west side (then nos. 13–17), not quite at right angles. The fourth side was never

Mr Wontner's House, Tibberton Square
The villa built by Thomas Wontner in 1808, in whose garden he created
Tibberton Square in 1827. The houses shown were demolished in 1896 to
make way for Greenman Street Baths
From a water-colour by Frederick N. Shepherd

built on, but was closed by ornamental railings and wrought-iron gates like the exclusive Highbury Place, leaving a vista to the south-east.

The family villa was attractively fanciful, its central front door flanked by Venetian windows with large shutters, another pair of Venetian windows on the first floor, and two 'thermal' windows or lunettes on the top floor above a broad string-course.

From the square's first occupation, in 1827, Wontner's sons and daughters lived at no. 28 until long after their father's death. The last daughter, Rebecca, died there, unmarried, in 1859. Thomas junior, who succeeded his father in the business and died without issue in 1851, was followed by his brother Joseph, whose son Algernon, a stockbroker, inherited in 1867.

By the 1870s the area was under pressure for building, with Peabody Square built in four blocks in 1866 and Greenman Street from 1873. In 1894 ground was required for building public swimming-baths under the Baths and Wash-Houses Act (1846–7), and unfortunately the whole west side of Tibberton Square, including the Wontner villa, was razed. The new baths on the site were opened in 1895. Perhaps for this reason, in 1896 the rest of the square was sold, as nos. 1–12 and 18–29, for £8,645. Later members of the Wontner family tried, unsuccessfully, to re-acquire any of the property.

The houses now went down in the world. Like much other local property they came into multiple occupation, and during the Second World War the enclosing gates and screen were pointlessly removed, as were most railings at the time, for illusory scrap metal collection.

Although the square's worth was recognised by its inclusion in 1968 in the St Peter's Ward conservation area, by 1970 only three of its houses were in single-family occupation, 46 households had no baths, and 28 no water supply. In January 1970 the square was acquired by the Council as one of 19 streets designated for face-lift, and restoration was carried out by the architects Andrews Sherlock & Partners, and the building group D. J. Higgins & Sons Ltd, and completed in June 1979.

The size of the houses made them inconvenient for single families, yet too small for conversion into individual flats. The 24 houses were therefore converted laterally, leaving the elevations unaltered, to make 36 two-bedroom flats and 12 one-bedroom, accommodating 132 persons. The central sloping garden was newly landscaped, and levelled by several feet at the western end to admit light to the dark basements. The railings were renewed. Parking was banned, and access to the two terraces limited to pedestrians. By the conversion, which cost £850,000, alternate front doors gave access to the ground floor and to the stair. The completed conversion was one of nine in the London area highly commended in a DOE competition (1980). It was opened in July 1979 by Merlyn Rees, one-time Home Secretary. Among those present was Thomas Wontner's great-great-great-grandson Sir Hugh Wontner, former Lord Mayor, chairman of Claridge's and the

Berkeley Hotels and a past Master of both the Worshipful Company of Feltmakers and the Worshipful Company of Clockmakers.

Sir Hugh's son Giles Wontner is senior partner of the City firm of solicitors Wontner & Sons, of Broad Court, Bow Street, founded by another Thomas Wontner who was grandson to the Tibberton Square Thomas's brother John. Thus the two branches of the family unite in the head of that firm.

Some years later the Greenman Street Baths themselves were closed and demolished, and in 1987 Wontner Close, a group of flats designed by the Council's Architects' Department, was built on part of the site, merging agreeably with the end of the square. The heights are pleasantly varied, and an interesting central staircase cleaves through a rift in the main building. West of the flats, the iron trusses from one of the swimming baths have been left in situ, and, painted a bright blue, greatly enhance the small recreation ground created on the rest of the space.

Architecture
Starkish: 3 storeys and basements, in brick, no stucco, no window-guards. Fronts are plain except the broad course above the basement. Ground-floor windows are round-headed, fanlights are the wreath-like double circle studded with florets, framed by tear-drop segments – frequent in Barnsbury and a simplification of the Bedford Way, Bloomsbury type. Those on the south side are renewals, but without florets.

The blind east fronts are finished with blank window recesses (cf. Arundel Square), and entrances to the end houses are placed on these fronts, except for no. 13 on the NW corner (the north terrace was re-numbered to run consecutively, 13–24. The terraces are raised on steps due to the fall in ground level from west to east. The backs, with only tiny gardens or yards, are rather more barrack-like than the average Islington terrace.

Inhabitants
Several of the Wontner family: 1852 Joseph Wontner (son), no. 28 Mrs Wontner; Rebecca Wontner (daughter) until 1859. In 1851/2 at no. 11 lived Richard Braine, great-grandfather to Sir Bernard Braine, MP (b. 1914): he died there aged 55 in 1852, and his wife and daughter continued to live there for a time.

Union Square (1851–52)
(see Arlington Square)

Union Square, straddling the boundary between the Clothworkers' and Packington estates, was built for Henry Rydon, starting with nos. 1 and 2, 1851, between Rydon and St Paul Streets, and most of the east side completed by 1852. The builders appear to have been Job Palmer, Edmund Barker and others, or at least they were first lessees. It was oddly laid out, effectively consisting only of the two long E and W

Union Square in 1957
East side (nos. 3-15) before the remainder was demolished to build the new
Packington estate. The houses are similar to those in Arlington Square

sides, the other two sides being 'incidental' – the south belonging to Linton Street
and the rest of the north side being partly filled by the narrow block between Canon
and Rector Streets.

In 1946 the London & Manchester Assurance Company presented the freehold to
Islington Council. In 1966 the square was, unhappily, sliced in two by the Council,
despite vigorous local protests, ruthlessly felling its west side (12 houses) along with
neighbouring streets, for rebuilding of the Packington estate. Only nos. 1–15
remain. (For the full implications of this see *Packington Square*).

The gardens were unaffected by the demolition and reinstated by the Council,
though for some years threatened with development by being included in a new
school site under the 1950s plan. They had been proposed for public access as far
back as 1908, when the Metropolitan Public Gardens Association was asked to
convert them to a park, the area being then even poorer than before and still densely
populated.

Architecture
The surviving east side (nos. 3–15), three storeys and basements and with rectangular features and ground floors stuccoed to first-floor level, echoes Arlington Square,

though here fewer window-guards remain. Front doors are distinguished by paired round-headed panels. The only built ornament is the bracketed mouldings of the first-floor windows.

North and south sides conform to the style and smaller scale of the surrounding streets. On the short north side, Palmer's nos.1 and 2 Union Square, and no. 80 St Paul Street, form a single bijou terrace: two storeys and basement with cornice, segmental door-case and windows, and window-guards. The south side, part of un-stuccoed Linton Street (1850), has segmental window-heads and the simple triangular door-pediments, doll's-house style, of most of the rest of the estate. The flat fronts and low-rise houses, with the unusually wide roadways, contribute to the generally spacious effect throughout the estate.

Wilton Square (1852–3)
(see also Arlington Square)

In 1812, with the forging of the New North Road through-route to the City, an awkwardly-shaped plot was isolated from the eastern edge of the Clothworkers' Estate. Some 35 years later, when building began on the estate, the only prospect for this site was for houses ranged round a central space – not even a square, but a triangle. Wilton Square bid fair to be the first site completed, when Richard Field, the lessee, who was a printer and "a commission agent for bandanas", signed an agreement to build 21 houses in New North Road (nos. 138–176), and Wilton Square itself.

Application was made to lay sewers and house drains, and between August 1846 and April 1847 the New North Road houses in three batches of seven, presumably in carcase, were leased to Field, who was also developing two plots round (now demolished) Basire Street to the north of the estate. For the New North Road houses he obtained leases in 1848, but did not complete the Wilton Square plot, and in 1849 he withdrew, assigning the other property to a relative while the Wilton Square site reverted to the Clothworkers. In 1851 or '2 it was leased to Edward Rowland and Thomas Evans, who were Rydon's sub-lessees in St Paul Street and Arlington Square, and it was Rowland and Evans who now built Wilton Square and Street.

The new square was first occupied in 1853. It was entered from the west by the narrow Wilton Street (since 1940 renamed Wilton Villas) off New North Road, with an exit to what is now Baring Street at the E tip of the triangle. The central space was occupied by a small Baptist chapel known as Salem, removed from Hoxton: it appears to have been preceded by a temporary chapel in 1847, and was rebuilt in 1866. A second, Welsh Methodist chapel was built by 1857 on the junction with Wilton Street.

Salem Chapel closed in 1913, and in 1931 the Clothworkers' Company sold it to the London & Manchester Insurance Company. Thenceforward it was used by the

Wilton Square in 1966, from Wilton Villas
showing the Welsh Methodist Chapel (1857), demolished 1960s.
Nos. 19-23, seen in the distance, are post-war infilling with no attempt to
match the original style

YMCA for some 30 years until 1963, after which it became derelict and vandalised, and was demolished. Meanwhile the Methodist chapel, rebuilt in 1884 to accommodate a schoolroom below, was restored in 1955 to serve as a hostel for the Catholic St Vincent's Housing Association. It has now been replaced by a purpose-built block by David Parry (1986), four storeys plus a recessed attic floor; brick with buttresses supporting a galleried 3rd floor with yellow metal windows. Glass canopies over entrance and small balconies. A quite attractive effect, but top-heavy, geared in scale to New North Road rather than the low square houses.

By the 1960s cars and lorries were using the square as a short cut via Baring Street to Hackney and in 1971 the entrance from New North Road was closed to traffic. In 1970 the gardens were replanted with a new layout, retaining the mature plane trees, new shrubs were planted and the railings were replaced.

Architecture
The shape is strictly a truncated triangle, with a short fourth side (6 houses) on the north. Unlike Arlington and Union Squares, Wilton Square was built on the modest scale of two storeys and basement suited to its restricted width. Its features are a

Wilton Square looking south, *c*. 1966
showing the façade of the Methodist chapel. Salem Chapel, originally in the
central gardens, was demolished in 1963

heavy horizontal cornice, segmental windows and plain triangular-pedimented
doorheads carried on brackets. In the north angle between nos. 10 and 11 is a pend
leading through wooden doors to a yard. At the east angle a space was left between
nos. 40 and 41, with lean-to buildings, doubtless workshops, attached and other
small buildings dotted about behind. During the Second World War nos. 40 and 41
and their appendages were bombed – as were nos. 19–23 on the NE side and the
Baring Street corner – and the space has been left open with trees, a car park and a
large Council building behind. Nos. 19–23 were rebuilt in a dreary, flat 1950s style,
and Stocks Lodge opposite, incorporating nos. 27A and 28, is a faceless box (1962).
Otherwise, apart from the loss of a pediment on no. 27 and cornice mouldings on
nos. 35 and 39, the houses externally have suffered little change. No. 30 alone has an
added modern attic.

Nos. 22A and B of the now eccentrically three-legged Baring street are a 1980s
infilling with a pair of low, cottage houses in pastiche 1850s style, with pretty
latticed iron porches, designed by the Borough Council Architects' Department.

With Wilton Villas now closed to traffic, the 'square' has become a quiet enclave
approached by car only from Baring Street, in atmosphere not unlike Granville
Square in Clerkenwell.

NOT SQUARES

A round-up of anomalies with little right to inclusion in the main list, their appearance and even existence being barely recognisable. Although for some reason appearing briefly in Rate Books boasting the name of 'square', they were either not squares but small terraces or even closes, or were early renamed, perhaps hardly developed. One or two, like Queen's Square, might have been intended for extension into a square proper, as had happened to Claremont Square in Pentonville, but were withered at birth. They are:

Adelaide Square

The first joker in the pack, a small street in masquerade, almost undocumented and non-recorded. It appears in the Rate Books from 1844–56, and was in fact a kind of service lane between Shepperton Street and South Street, one of those rhomboidal islands adjoining the Clothworkers' estate enclosing enough space to contain a further strip of building. The row of some half-dozen tenements (as the Rate Books show) was entered through a pend in Shepperton Street, with a National School, run by St Barnabas' Church, tucked in to the north. Its appearance is unknown, as is the excuse for calling it a 'square'.

South Street (1848) was renamed Basire Street in 1938, and "Adelaide Square" became part of it although still noted in the Directory in 1940. In 1972 the whole block was demolished and rebuilt as Council housing.

Albert Square, Highbury Corner (1854)

This is another non-starter, possibly similar to such courts as Adelaide and Compton Squares, though the early map does show a square-like area. It was behind Swan Yard, which belonged to the Old White Swan formerly at 13 Holloway Road, is listed in Censuses from 1861–81, and appears on the large-scale OS 1871 map just south of Highbury Station. In 1867, however, the North London Railway acquired the site, on the edge of existing railway land, and closed the adjoining Albert Street.

Cobden Square, Islington High Street

One more in the category of Compton Square: in the warren of tiny courts and alleys off the east side of the High Street, between the Angel and the Back Road. It is shown unnamed as early as Greenwood's map of 1835, but evidently regarded as too mean

Edward's Cottages, off Canonbury Road, in 1955
These cottages, demolished in 1956, were similar in size and style to Compton Square

to figure in Directories; nor does it figure in Rate Books. In the 1871 Ordnance Survey it is dignified with a name commemorating the MP Richard Cobden (1804–65), Anti-Corn Law and pro-Free Trade campaigner. In the 1870s the whole Angel rookery was condemned and cleared, Cobden Square included.

Compton Square

A narrow entry just north of the junction of Compton Avenue with Canonbury Road. South of the junction was the "British School" which Union Chapel had opened in 1807 for girls and in 1814 also for boys, and which moved to its present site from a room behind the Chapel in 1868. In 1873 it was transferred to the new London School Board, and became the Canonbury Road (now Canonbury) School. North of this until World War II was a rash of cottages, and in line with the rear of 23 Compton Terrace an alley opened into "Compton Square", a small scattered group which might just be deemed a square, abutting on the east on Keen's Yard leading off St Paul's Road. North of this again came Compton Mews, Goldsmith's Place, three more houses, and finally the Hen and Chickens pub at St Paul's Road corner.

Compton Square appears on the 1871 Ordnance Survey, and seems to have been one of the courts where cab drivers kept and serviced their vehicles, for on 4 October 1878 the Vestry Minutes record "a nuisance caused by cabs being washed and goats running about unrestrained in the square".

The whole corner was badly damaged by the V2 which destroyed the end of Compton Terrace (q.v.), and the battered remains of this group of alleys, still seen on the official War Damage map, were finally obliterated with the enlarging of Highbury Corner, and the building in 1966 of Dixon Clark Court.

Elder Square (1848) off Elder Walk, Lower Street

Appears in the Sewer Rate Book in 1848, with five houses under the name of Francis Weaver. Whatever it consisted of must have been small cottages. Elder Walk itself, dating from about 1800, was little more, one of several humble rows inhabited by workers in ancillary trades of the watch and clock industry. The term "square" may have meant only the spacing of cottages round a small court.

Norfolk Square

The most shadowy of these phantom squares, off New Norfolk Street (now Ecclesbourne Road); also near the Lower Road but considerably farther along, among the streets built on Thomas Scott's land (see Annett's Crescent). Although it appears in Rate Books between 1844 and 1855, it does not figure on maps, in printed Directories or even in sewer plans of the period. It too must have been only a short row of houses.

Also in this period, Concord Buildings appears in Rate Books between New Norfolk Street and Norfolk Square, and in the 1930s, when the LCC suppressed many old names as confusing duplications, Concord Buildings, Ecclesbourne Road, is noted as "Pulled down, part of Norfolk Square playground".

Queen's Square (Queensland Road) (1845)

This was merely a loop at the east end of Queen's (now Queensland) Road off what was to become Benwell Road, linking with Hornsey Road. The first Rate Books appearance is 1845. In 1848 the loop is listed as "Queen's Square", though Stanford's London and Suburbs map of 1862, and Cassell's *London* of the same date both show the south side of it as "Victoria Place" and the latter calls the north side "Queen's Place". There was a short alley exit eastwards to the temporary St Barnabas Church.

It could claim to be a 'square' only in the sense that it was evidently intended as central feature of a street which would continue eastwards and link with the proposed Drayton Park. The railway later intervened, however, and thus it became a cul-de-sac, doubling back on itself so that one went out by the way one had come in.

This feature of the street probably contributed to its reputation, by the end of the century, as one of Islington's most notorious hot-spots, occupied by families of the underworld, second in crime only to Campbell Road, and entered by the police only in pairs, or even threes.

In 1872 Queen's Road was renamed Queensland Road, and in 1940 this was extended to include the loop. From 1957 onwards the area was cleared by the LCC. For some years past it has consisted entirely of industrial buildings, with not a house remaining.

Suggested routes for walks

Barnsbury and Canonbury
(Starting from the Angel)

    Cloudesley Square
    Gibson Square
    Milner Square
    Lonsdale Square
    Barnsbury Square
    Thornhill Square
    Arundel Square
    (Highbury Corner)
    Compton Terrace
    Canonbury Square
    Alwyne Square/John Spencer Square

It is impossible to visit the Barnsbury squares in chronological order without considerable back-tracking.

St Peter's Ward and the eastern squares
(Starting from Islington Green)

    Packington Square
    Union Square
    Arlington Square
    Wilton Square
    Tibberton Square
    Peabody Square
    Annett's Crescent

Highbury
(Starting from Highbury Corner)

    Highbury Place
    Highbury Terrace
    (diversion to) Highbury Park Terrace
    Highbury Crescent

Colebrooke Row and Duncan Terrace contain enough to make an expedition in themselves.

Chronological List of the Squares of Islington
(Dates of first building)

Colebrooke Row	Early 18th century and 1768–1841
Highbury Place	1774–9
Highbury Terrace	1789–94 and 1817
Duncan Terrace	1791–1841
Compton Terrace	1805–9, 1819–31
Canonbury Square	1805–9, 1821–30, 1954
Annett's Crescent	1822–6
Cloudesley Square	1826
Barnsbury Square	1827, 1835–44
Tibberton Square	1827
Highbury Park Terrace	1829, 1831–6
Gibson Square	1831, 1836–9
Malvern Terrace	1836–8
Lonsdale Square	1838–45
Highbury Crescent	1844–50
Milner Square	1841–7
Thornhill Square	1847–9, 1851–2
Arlington Square	1849–51
Arundel Square	1850–60
Union Square	1851–2
Wilton Square	1852–3
Edward Square	1853
Alwyne Square	1857–63, 1954
Peabody Square	1866
Peckett Square and Taverner Square	1922
John Spencer Square	1963
Packington Square	1966–70
Cornwallis Square	1988–90
Angel Square	1991

BIBLIOGRAPHY

Particular items or squares for which certain works were consulted are identified by the following abbreviations or initials (of squares, unless otherwise noted):

Int	Introduction	HPk	Highbury Park Terrace
Al	Alwyne	HP	Highbury Place
An	Angel	HT	Highbury Terrace
Ann	Annett's Crescent	J	John Spencer
A	Arlington	L	Lonsdale
Ar	Arundel	MT	Malvern Terrace
B	Barnsbury	M	Milner
C	Canonbury	P	Packington
C/D	Colebrooke Row/Duncan Terrace	Pb	Peabody
Cl	Cloudesley	P/T	Peckett/Taverner
Co	Compton Terrace	Th	Thornhill
Co/U	Do., Union Chapel	T	Tibberton
Cw	Cornwallis	U	Union
E	Edward	W	Wilton
G	Gibson	NS	Not Squares
HC	Highbury Crescent		

The following general sources were consulted for the majority of squares and terraces dealt with in this book:

Special Collections

Greater London Record Office (GLRO):
  Holborn & Finsbury Commissioners for Sewers: Rate Books and Minute Books (HFCS)
  Middlesex Deeds Register (MDR)
  St Mary's Islington Parish Registers

London Division of English Heritage:
  Islington reports by former GLC and now English Heritage London Region historians:
No. 5	Milner Square (Susan Beattie, 1971)	
No. 6	Canonbury (Hubert Bennett, 1965)	
No. 10	Colebrooke Row, Duncan Terrace and Charlton Place (Frank Kelsall, 1966)	
No. 20	Clothworkers' Estate (Frank Kelsall, 1967)	

No. 27   Highbury Place, no. 24, and Highbury Terrace (Frank Kelsall, 1972)
No. 32   Highbury Crescent (Frank Kelsall, 1973)
No. 99   Highbury Place, nos. 13–15 (Alan Crawford, 1989)
No. 161   Liverpool Road, no. 90 (Edward Chaney, 1991)

Islington Central Libraries, Local History Collection:
  Cuttings collection
  Highbury Terrace Residents' Association Minute Book, 1812–34
  Rate Books
  Richard Dent's Survey of the Parish of Islington, 1805/6
  Trustees of Committee of Highways & Footpaths, Minute Books, 1830–36
  Vestry Minute Books, 1833–37

Maps and printed books:
  London Directories (Robson's, Kelly's, Post Office) in Greater London and
    Guildhall Libraries
  Maps: Dent's Survey (see above), Horwood, 1799, Cruchley, 1829, Greenwood
    1835, Stanford, London & Suburbs, 1862, Ordnance Survey, 1871 and 2nd
    World War Damage map
  Nelson's (1811 & 1829) and Lewis's (1842) *Histories of Islington* and Cromwell's
    Walks Through Islington (1835)
  Tomlins, Thomas Edlyn, *Perambulation of Islington*, 1858
  Victoria County History, Middlesex Vol. VIII, University of London Institute of
    Historical Research, 1985 (VCH)
  Willats, Eric, *Streets with a Story*, Islington Local History Trust, 2nd edn, 1988

General list of Books and Articles

The Ambulator, 1820 etc.   B
The A to Z of Victorian London, ed. Ralph Hyde, London Topographical Society, 1981
Barnsbury Wood, London Borough of Islington, 1984, and *The Future of Barnsbury
  Wood*, Barnsbury Wood Co-operative, 1981   B
Bennison, Peter, *The Development of the Thornhill Estate*, unpublished dissertation for
  the Architectural Association School of Architecture, 1978   Th
Black, Kenneth MacLeod, *The Scots Churches in London*, 1906   C/D
Cassell's London, 1862   NS (Queen's)
Colvin, Howard, *A Biographical Dictionary of British Architects, 1600–1840*, John
  Murray, 1981   Ann, C/D, G, HP, L, M
Connoisseur, The, 1767   C/D
Flashback, publications for Islington Borough Council (including Union Chapel,
  1987)   Co/U

Forbes-Robertson, Sir Johnston, *A Player under Three Reigns*, 1925   B
Charles Lamb Society Bulletin, NS 30, April 1980   C/D
Gillo, Joseph, *Bibliographical Dictionary of the English Catholics*, 1885   C/D
Hearn, Nicholas, *George Peabody (1795–1869)*, Dulwich College O Level History
    Project, 1981 (reprinted 1990 for Peabody Trust)   Pb
Hobhouse, Hermione, *Thomas Cubitt, Master Builder*, Macmillan, 1971   C/D, G, M
Hone, William, *The Every-Day Book*, 3 vols., 1827   B
Letters of Charles Lamb, ed. E. V. Lucas, 3 vols., 1935   C/D
Lewis, Thomas, *A Retrospect of the Moral and Religious State of Islington, during the last
    40 Years. A Sermon*, delivered to Union Chapel . . . August 28, 1840; 1842   A
Low's Handbook to the Charities of London, 1889–1900, ed. H. R. Dumville, 1900   C/D
Lysons, Daniel, *London and its Environs*, 1792–1811   B
Marrs, Edwin W., jr, *Letters of Charles and Mary Lamb*, 3 vols., Cornell University,
    1978 ff.   C/D
Martin, B. E., *In the Footsteps of Charles Lamb*,   C/D
Peabody Trust, 1862–1987, p.p. for the Trust, 1987   Pb
Pevsner, Nicholas, *London except the Cities of London and Westminster*, Buildings of
    England series, 1951
Rottmann, Alexander, *London's Catholic Churches*, 1926   C/D
Sugden, Keith, *History of Highbury*, Islington Archaeology & History Society,
    1984   HPk
Summerson, Sir John, *Georgian London*, 1945 edn   M
Temple, Philip, *Islington Chapels*, Royal Commission on the Historical Monuments of
    England, 1992   C/D, Co/U, HP, M, W
Tibberton Square 1839–1979, London Borough of Islington Architects' Dept,
    1979   T
Union Chapel: Co/U
    History of Union Chapel, A, p.p. for Friends of Union Chapel, 1988
    Union Chapel: The Story of a Hundred Years 1799–1899, 1899
    Various accounts published by Friends of Union Chapel, London Borough of
    Islington Economic Development Unit, Save Britain's Heritage, the Victorian
    Society, etc.
Whatley, Stephen, *England's Gazetteer*, 1756   B
Whittaker, C. R., *The Thornhill Estate in Islington*, unpublished thesis for the
    University of London, 1959   Th

Periodicals

The Builder, 1855, 1946   A
Country Life, 1939   M
Crossbow, summer 1976   P

The Draper, 1869   Th
The Ecclesiologist, 1854, 1856   Th, A
Evening Standard, 18 Sept., 1969   P
The Gentleman's Magazine, Jan. 1799, May 1829, 1909   C/D, Cl, B
Illustrated London News, 1854   Th
Islington Gazette, 1934, 1992   B, An, Cw, P
Oracle, The, 3 July 1792   HP
Sydney Morning Herald, Sept. 1961   Ann

INDEX

Charke Charlotte, née Cibber 55
Charke, Richard, violinist 55
Charlecote Estates 5
Charles Street, Gibson Square 92, 94, 97
Charlton Crescent 9, 50, 58, 77
Charlton Place 50, 58, 60, 77
Charterhouse School 36
Charterhouse Square 1
Chartist Movement 64
Chelsea Physic Garden 52
chimneys, industrial 31, 139
Christ Church, Highbury 124
church attendance 17, 49, 66, 82-3, 143
church building 12, 15, 49, 64-7, 124, 140
Church Commissioners, see Ecclesiastical
   Commissioners
churches and chapels: see Algiers, English church
   at; All Saints, Battle Bridge; Barnsbury
   Chapel; Catholic Apostle Church (Irvingite
   Church); Celestial Church of Christ (formerly
   Holy Trinity); Chapel of Ease (St Mary
   Magdalene); Christ Church, Highbury;
   Claremont Chapel, Pentonville; Countess of
   Huntingdon's Chapel, City; Evangelical
   Brotherhood Chapel, Highbury Place; Glasite
   (see Sandemanian); Greenwich Roman
   Catholic Chapel; Grove Road, Chapel of Our
   Lady; Hatton Garden meeting house; Holy
   Trinity, Cloudesley Square; Irvingite (later
   Catholic Apostolic Church); Islington
   Presbyterian Church; King's College Chapel,
   Cambridge; Lancing College Chapel; London
   Presbyterian Church of Scotland (see
   Islington Presbyterian Church); Milner
   Square, proposed church; Our Lady, Chapel
   of (see Grove Road); Pentecostal Church (see
   Celestial Church of Christ); Providence
   Chapel, Highbury Place; Providence Chapel,
   Islington Green; St Andrew's; St Barnabas;
   St Bartholomew's, Smithfield; St Botolph's,
   Aldersgate; St Clement's, Barnsbury;
   St Clement's basilica, Rome; St David's,
   Cardiff; St David's, Westbourne Road;
   St Gile's Cripplegate; St James's,
   Chillingworth Road; St James's, Prebend
   Street; St John of Jerusalem, Clerkenwell;
   St John's, Hackney; St John's, Hoxton;
   St John's, Upper Holloway; St John the
   Evangelist Roman Catholic Church; St Luke's,
   Chelsea; St Mark's, Clerkenwell; St Mary

Magdalene, Chapel of Ease; St Mary's,
   Islington; St Matthew's, Essex Road;
   St Matthias, Caledonian Road; St Paul's
   Cathedral; St Paul's, Ball's Pond; St Peter's,
   Stonyhurst College; St Philip the Evangelist,
   Arlington Square; St Stephen's, Canonbury;
   St Thomas, Hemingford Road; St Thomas,
   Regent Street; Salem Baptist Chapel, Wilton
   Square; Sandemanian (Glasite) meeting house;
   Santa Fosca, Torcello; Scottish Presbyterian
   (see Islington Presbyterian); temporary iron
   churches; Union Chapel; Ward's Place, Lower
   Street; Welsh Methodist Chapel, Wilton
   Square; Westminster Cathedral
Cibber, Charlotte, see Charke, Charlotte
Cibber, Colly 55
Circle 33 Housing Trust 18, 86
City of London 6, 12, 37, 51, 59, 60, 110, 146,
   151
City Parochial Foundation 14, 129
City Road 10, 51, 58, 59, 65, 69, 70, 75, 79
City Road Basin 59, 60
Civic Trust 130
Claremont Chapel, Pentonville 110
Claremont Close, Pentonville 3
Claremont Square 2, 3, 64, 154
Clay Pit Field 58
Clayton & Bell, stained glass by 20
Clerkenwell 1, 2, 3, 43, 47, 55, 64, 79, 120
Clerkenwell County Court 51, 65, 78
Clerkenwell Green 2
clock, presentation, Union Chapel 83
clock and watch trade, workers in 156
Clothworkers' Company 10, 12, 14, 38
Clothworkers' Company Corporate Estate 2,
   10-17 passim, 51-2, 129, 149-51, 154
Cloudesley, Sir Richard 45, 49
Cloudesley estate (14 Acres or Stonefield estate)
   2, 26, 44-47, 92
Cloudesley Place (formerly Elizabeth Terrace) 46,
   47
Cloudesley Road (formerly Upper & Lower
   Islington Terrace) 26, 46, 47
Cloudesley Square 2, 3, 15, 41, 44-9 passim, 118
Cloudesley Street 46, 47
Cloudesley Terrace 44, 92
coach-houses 4, 31, 102, 104, 106, 108, 109, 113
Coade stone 77, 79, 113
Cobden, Richard, MP 155
Cobden Square, Islington High Street, 154-5

Drayton Park 157; station 104
Ducie, Sir Hugh 135
Ducie, Sir Robert, Lord Mayor 135
"Duke of Shoreditch", archery target 10
"Duncan Place" (1-3 Colebrooke Row) 50, 59, 75
Duncan Place (Duncan Terrace) 59
Duncan Street 51, 52, 60, 63, 67, 78
Duncan Terrace 2, 3, 49-70 passim, 75-9 passim, 102
Dyer, George, poet 60

earthworks, Barnsbury and Highbury 22-24, 25-6, 31; see also Reed Moat Field
East Street (now Eastney Street), Greenwich 58
East India Company 114; Office 62
East India Docks 114
Eastwyke Field, architects 108
Ecclesbourne Road (formerly New Norfolk Street) 3, 156
Ecclesiastical Commissioners 12, 13, 14, 47
Ecclesiologist, The, quoted 15, 143
Eddington, John, nurseryman 53
Edgbaston, Birmingham 85
Edinburgh 64
Edmonton 62
Edward IV, King 52
Edward Square 2, 18, 87-8
Edward Terrace, Caledonian Road 87, 88
Edwards, Francis, architect 89, 92, 93, 95
Edwards, Thomas, lexicographer 49
Elder Square, Lower Street 156
Elder Walk, Lower Street 156
Eley, William, Northampton Lodge 41
Elia Street (formerly Alfred Street) 66, 74
Elizabeth I, Queen 37
Elizabeth Fry Home for Girls, see homes and hostels
Elizabeth Terrace, see Cloudesley Place
Ellington Street 20
Elmore Street (formerly James Street) 6
Elrington, Sir John 52
Emmett, John, builder and carpenter 46
Enfield 62
England, Louis, timber merchant and builder 25, 92
England's Gazetteer, see Whatley, Stephen
Englefield Road 8
English & French Dyeing Co. Ltd 31
English Heritage 83
Environment, Department of the 133

Erith, Raymond, architect 95
Essex Road (Lower Road) 2, 5, 6, 8, 14, 15, 51
Essex Road Branch Railway 60
estates: see Canonbury; Clothworkers' Company, Corporate Estate; Cloudesley (14 Acres, Stonefield); Drapers' Company; Foundling Estate; Milner-Gibson; Mountfort; New River Company; Northampton; Packington; Prebend; Taverner; Thornhill; Wenlock Barn
Eton House, Leigh Road 102
Evangelical Brotherhood Church, Highbury Place 106, 108
Evans, Thomas, builder 13, 14, 151
Evening Standard, quoted 44
Everilda Street 139

factories: beer bottling 6, 9; dyeing 31; floor-cloth manufacturing 6, 9; furs for hats 146; mica 31, 34; soap 135; soda water 62; white lead 6
fanlights 9, 17, 36, 43, 75, 77, 78, 79, 81, 101, 108, 113, 149
Felix Place, Liverpool Road 89, 92
Felix Terrace, Liverpool Road 89
Feltmakers, Worshipful Company of 146
Felton, Robert, seed merchant 100
Field, Richard, printer 151
Fieldway Crescent 98
Fincham, Henry W., Librarian, Order of St John 44
Finsbury, borough of 1, 2
Finsbury Circus 13
Finsbury Fields 10, 66
Finsbury Park 136
Finsbury Square 129
Fire of London 1
Fisher family 1
Fitzroy Square 75
Fletcher, Geoffrey, artist 129
Fletcher, George Rutter, FSA, solicitor 129
Fletcher, Hanslip, artist 129
Flower, Henry, builder, Clerkenwell 79, 81
footman's room 104, 405
Forbes-Robertson family 31, 36
Forbes-Robertson, John 36
Forbes-Robertson, Sir Johnston 24, 31, 36
Foster, W. M. B. & Sons, beer bottlers 6, 9
Foster Probyn Ltd, beer bottlers 6, 9
Foundling Estate, Bloomsbury 138
fountain, Barnsbury Square 33
Fourteen Acres Estate, see Cloudesley Estate

parking problem 46, 93
Parliamentary debates, reporting of 57
Parliamentary road, see Caledonian Road
Parry, David, architect 152
"Patrol", Highbury Terrace 114
Peabody, George, philanthropist 133
Peabody Donation Fund 133, 135
Peabody House 133
Peabody Square 133-6 passim, 148
Peachey, James, land-owner 86
Peckett, George, Vestryman 136
Peckett Square 136
pediments 17, 93, 95, 127, 153
Penn Road 3
Pentecostal Church (formerly Holy Trinity), see
    Celestial Church of Christ
Pentonville 2, 3, 22, 64, 111, 136
Pentonville Hill 59
Pentonville Prison 18, 139
Perkins, John, market director 6, 8
Peto, Henry, Highbury Terrace 115
Pevsner, Sir Nikolaus, quoted 57
Phelps, Samuel, actor-manager 36, 44
Pied Bull inn 89
Pilgrim Fathers 85; Society of America 85
Pitcairn, Dr William 89, 124
Pite, E. Beresford, architect 140, 143
plaques and tablets, commemorative 24, 66, 79;
    terrace names/dates 43, 46, 55, 58, 73, 77
pleasure gardens 26, 37, 139
Plymouth rock, at Union Chapel 85
Pocock family 18, 22, 151
Pocock, George 89
Pocock, Richard 18
Pocock, Samuel 18, 139, 140
Pocock's Fields 18
Poetical Blossoms, or *The Sports of Genius* 55
police flats, Canonbury Park South 4
police station, Colebrooke Row, see Old Court
    House
Pond Field 24-5
ponds 92, 94
Poole, Dr Robert, smallpox hospital 135
Poole Street, Hackney 14
population decrease 17, 66, 83, 88, 142; increase
    14, 15, 26, 47, 49, 124, 140
porches and porticoes 30, 34, 35, 36, 43, 71, 73,
    81, 82, 98, 100, 101, 106, 108, 109, 113, 127,
    142
"Praetorium", see Reed Moat Field

Prebble & Co., estate agents 118
Prebend estate 10, 51
Prebend Street 17, 129, 133
Prebendal manor 51
Presbyterian church, see Islington Presbyterian
    church
Presbyterian Church of Scotland 64, 65
Pring, Kenneth, architect 127
Prior Bolton Street 116
Priory Villas, see Canonbury Park South
private schools, see schools
Probyn, Mr A., beer bottler 6
proprietary schools, see schools
Prospect Cottages, Minerva Road (38-60
    Thornhill Road) 25, 26
prosperity, decline in Islington 31, 40, 93, 118,
    124, 150
Providence Chapel, Highbury Place 110
Providence Chapel, Islington Green 109
Pryde, Mr D. I., Inspector, Packington Public
    Enquiry 131
Public Gardens, Boulevards and Playgrounds
    Association 43
Public Advertiser, 57
public houses, renaming of 5, 8
Pugin, Augustus Welby Northmore, architect 67,
    118
Pugsley, Charles, manufacturer 6
Pullin family 53, 66

Queen's Place, see Queen's Square
Queen's Square (now Queensland Road)
    (formerly Queen's Place & Victoria Place)
    156-7
Queensbury Street 3
Queensland Road (formerly Queen's Road) 156-7

Ragged School, Lower Street 135
railings 43, 47, 77, 96, 97, 118, 148
railways 60
Raleigh, Sir Walter 89
Ramage, Mr, builder, see Stevenson & Ramage
Rate Books, see Islington Rate Books
rates, parish 114-5, 116
Ray, Cyril, connoisseur 59
Rector Street 13, 129, 133, 150
Red Lion Street, Holborn 79
Redspring, development company 118
Reed Moat Field ("Praetorium") 22-3, 24, 25; see
    also Pond Field, Barnsbury

Gibson, Granville, John Spencer, Lonsdale, Milner, Norfolk, Packington, Peabody, Peckett, Powys, Queen's (= Queensland Road), St John's, Taverner, Thornhill, Tibberton, Union, Wilmington and Wilton Squares; see also Annett's Crescent; Colebrooke Row/Duncan Terrace; Compton Terrace; Highbury Crescent, Park Terrace, Place and Terrace; Malvern Cottages/Terrace
squares, style of building in Islington 4, 17, 20, 28, 41, 43, 46, 47, 86, 93-5, 116, 118, 120, 126, 127, 133, 135-6, 142, 149, 150-1, 152-3
stables 31, 46, 104, 109, 115
stained glass 20, 49, 85
Stamford Street, Lambeth, Peabody Buildings 135
Stanford's map, 1862 156
Starvation Farm 54, 75
steam tug, Regent's Canal 59-60
Steemson, Samuel, carpenter 52, 71
Stevenson & Ramage, builders 64
Stoke Newington 38, 70
Stokes, Mr, Essex Road 43
Stonefield Estate, see Cloudesley estate
Stonefield Street 46, 49, 118
Stonyhurst College, Lancs 67
Strand, The 57
street sweepers 114
stuccoing 9, 17, 20, 34, 35, 36, 41, 43, 47, 50, 71, 73, 77, 78, 81, 93, 98, 100, 101, 108, 109, 116, 127, 142, 150
Studd Street 89, 92
Sturt's Lock, Regent's Canal 14
Suess, Edward, economist 79
"Suetonius Lodge" 28
Suetonius Paulinus 22-3
Summerson, Sir John, quoted 124
Sun Row, Lower Street 135
Sunday School, Union Chapel 85
Swan Yard, Holloway Road 154
swimming-baths and pools 11, 148, 149
Swinburne, Algernon Charles 36
Swinton Street, Gray's Inn Road 25
Sydney Morning Herald, quoted 10
Sydenham 54

Tasker, Francis William, architect 67, 69
Taverner, Louis, Highbury Grange 136
Taverner Estate 136
Taverner Square 136
Taylor, James, surveyor and builder 50, 77

Taylor, Rev. Ronald 83
tea gardens, Oldfield's 26
Telecommunications Workshop, Holloway 86
"temple", Gibson Square, see ventilation shaft
temporary iron churches 15, 20, 82
tennis courts 33, 110
Terrace Field, Highbury 110
Terry, Quinlan, architect 95
Theberton Street 89, 92, 93, 123
Theobalds Road 64
Thompson, John, lessee 86
Thornhill, George 138
Thornhill, George, younger, MP 138, 140
Thornhill, Capt. Noel 142, 143
Thornhill Bridge, Regent's Canal 138
Thornhill Crescent 140, 142, 145
Thornhill estate 24, 45, 49, 121, 136, 138, 142
Thornhill Gardens (Malvern Terrace) 121, 122
Thornhill Road 25, 28, 31, 32, 35, 44, 121, 136, 138
Thornhill Square 2, 3, 17, 136-46 passim
Three Acres Field 66
Tibberton, Worcs. 146
Tibberton Square 2, 3, 6, 140, 146-9 passim
Tile-Kiln Field (= Hattersfield) 53, 71
Tirley Vicarage, Glos 30
Tollington 2
Tollington Way 86
Tomlins, Thomas Edlyne, 97; *A Perambulation of Islington*, quoted 10, 12, 24, 26, 28, 92, 94
Torcello 85
Tourle, J. F. 30
towers, church: St Andrew's 143; St John the Evangelist 67; St Philip the Evangelist 15; Union Chapel 85
Townsend, Mr, nurseryman 121
Trade, Board of 97
Transport, Minister of 95
Tregeer, William Henry and John Cornelius, academy 14n.
Trinidad 89
Trinidad Place, Liverpool Road 92, 121
Trinity House 114
Truefitt, George, architect 65
Tudor style 118, 120
Tufnell family 88
Tufnell Park 2
tunnel, Highgate Hill 59; New River 52; Regent's Canal, see Regent's Canal
Twickenham 54